Plug Into God's Rainbow

Plug Into God's Rainbow

Joyce K. Ellis

Zondervan Publishing House
Grand Rapids, Michigan

Daybreak Books are published by Zondervan Publishing House,
1415 Lake Drive, S.E., Grand Rapids, Michigan 49506

PLUG INTO GOD'S RAINBOW
Copyright © 1984 by The Zondervan Corporation
Grand Rapids, Michigan

Library of Congress Cataloging in Publication Data

Ellis, Joyce K.
  Plug into God's rainbow.

  1. Meditations. 2. Ellis, Joyce K.
I. Title.
BV4832.2.E37   1984   242   84-17584

ISBN 0-310-47192-3

Edited by Julie Ackerman Link
Designed by Ann Cherryman

Printed in the United States of America

84 85 86 87 88 89 / 10 9 8 7 6 5 4 3 2 1

*With love
to Marianne Ellis,
my wonderful mother-in-law*

Acknowledgments

The author is grateful for permission to quote from the following copyrighted sources:

Parts of chapter 6 are from "Miscarriage of Time." Reprinted by permission from the *Evangelical Beacon,* magazine of the Evangelical Free Church of America.

The gospel song quoted in chapter 7 is "Finally Home," © Copyright 1971 by Singspiration, Inc. All rights reserved. Used by permission.

Parts of chapter 9 are from "A Slight Dischord," from *The Church Musician,* March 1981, © Copyright 1981, The Sunday School Board of the Southern Baptist Convention. All rights reserved. Used by permission.

Unless otherwise indicated, Scripture is from the HOLY BIBLE: NEW INTERNATIONAL VERSION. Copyright © 1978 by the International Bible Society. Used by permission of Zondervan Bible Publishers.

Contents

Introduction

In today's fast-paced, high stress/low self-esteem world, we need somewhere to turn for help and something to offer us hope. Rainbows have been a symbol of hope for me. They have fascinated me ever since I was a little girl and heard the story of Noah's ark and watched Judy Garland on TV in *The Wizard of Oz*. Even though we had a black and white set, when she sang "Somewhere Over the Rainbow," I saw that rainbow in a splendor transcending technicolor.

Then in my junior year in high school I played the female lead in *Finian's Rainbow*. The song I enjoyed most, "Look to the Rainbow," is about a father who gives his daughter a song to sing whenever she feels the world is falling apart. He tells her to look to the rainbow as a symbol of encouragement. "Follow the fellow who follows a dream" is the last line. If I had written that song, I would have ended it: "Follow the fellow who shows you some hope." It doesn't rhyme, but a poetry instructor once told me never to let the rhyme get in the way of the message.

If there is any message we need today, it's *hope*. A week's worth of evening news or daily newspapers is enough to make a person O.D. on fright, discouragement, or panic.

There are times when my daily routine is so overscheduled that I feel like a roast that has been in the pressure cooker too long—charred and falling apart.

Personality conflicts, time battles, and household storms are sometimes so rough that I become wrapped up in a gloomy cloud of gray, and the tears flow as naturally as rain. That's why I like to surround myself with rainbows. A little rainbow decal on my windshield, a pin on my dress, a picture of a rainbow near my typewriter, all remind me to look in the Bible for God's promise for each new problem.

God doesn't want us to be unhappy. He came to give us life that is so full it overflows with His love and joy.

Surround yourself with rainbows! Surround yourself with God's promises.

Give me a rainbow, Lord—
A message of hope from You.
Show me within the storm clouds
That arc of delicate hue.

—Joyce K. Ellis

1 What Old Noah Saw

Rainbows are fascinating. They appear suddenly in all their indescribable beauty; they move with you as you drive down the highway; and they disappear as quickly as they come.

But even more interesting than a rainbow itself is its significance. Remember the story of Noah's ark and the parade of animals that marched up the plank two by two? After the storm God put a rainbow in the sky as a promise to Noah that He would never again destroy the entire earth with water—a promise He has kept ever since.

There are times, however, when floodwaters seem to be overtaking me and I begin to wonder if God can be trusted. Sometimes I remember an encouraging word of Scripture and try to hang on to it as if it were a lifeline from a rescue ship. But if the rescue doesn't come immediately, I let go and fall back into that familiar flood of self-pity. I've found many promises while reading the Bible. And I believe each of them—in my head, anyway. But in a crisis my first reaction is to panic.

I wonder if Noah suffered from "ark fever." And when the rain stopped, did he get impatient waiting several more months before the earth dried and he could finally get out of that zoo?

What about Mrs. Noah? Guess who probably did most of the cooking and cleaning? According to my calculations, she and her family spent a year and three days cooped up with at least two of every animal that existed! And by the end of that amount of time, there were probably more than two of every kind—especially rabbits. As many as 600 of them could have hopped out.

God had promised safety from destruction in the flood, and Noah obeyed all God told him to do. But didn't Noah get discouraged when the dove he released from the window came right back after finding no dry place to make a home? Didn't this godly, but normal, family begin to wonder if they'd ever again see dry land?

The Bible doesn't answer those questions for us, but we know two things. Noah was human. And "Noah found grace (favor NASB) in the eyes of the Lord."

No matter how tough it was, they *were inside!* Maybe the Noah family did get discouraged or depressed or impatient—maybe all three. But they were inside God's will and clung to God's promise for their safety. When they finally came out into the sunshine, Noah built an altar and offered a sacrifice, praising and thanking God.

God responded with the first rainbow of promise. God said, "I set My bow in the cloud, and it shall be for a sign of a covenant between Me and the earth. . . . never again shall the water become a flood to destroy all flesh. When the bow is in the cloud, then I will look upon it, to remember the everlasting covenant between God and every living creature of all flesh that is on the earth" (Genesis 9:13–16 NASB).

Wow! The rainbow is not only to remind us of

God's promises, but to remind Him (as if He needed reminding) what He has vowed.

But how do we get from knowing *about* God's promises to really experiencing them?

Not long ago, I was asked to sing at a small chapel in another city. The night before I was to sing, I sat on my bed deciding which cassette accompaniment tapes to use. I plugged the cord into the tape player and turned it on. Nothing happened. I fiddled with it for quite a while, panicking at the thought of no accompaniment. Finally, I realized that the cord wasn't plugged into the outlet—its power source.

Nice story, right? But promises are not something you can hold in your hand. Plugs with prongs and outlets I understand, but what's the power source for a rainbow promise? How can I "plug in" to a rainbow?

Red
Section

Anger

Anyone can become angry—that is easy, but to be angry with the right person, to the right degree, at the right time, for the right purpose, and in the right way—this is not easy.

—*Aristotle*

2 A Rainbow for Marital Tension

One of the best ways to illustrate the "plugging in" process is to relate some of the early stings of marital tension my husband and I felt.

No one had prepared me for the adjustments a person has to make in the early days of marriage. I thought our love would make Steve and me "one"—in immediate agreement on what to do, where to go, and how to live. Then my bubble burst!

One night my husband wanted to do one thing and I wanted to do another. (It was so important that I can't even remember what it was anymore.) I did the only calm, logical, female thing to do—I pouted. Quite predictably, he did the only normal, rational, male thing to do—he ignored me.

Of course nothing could have made me angrier. I stormed out of the house, waiting for him to do the only normal, *romantic* thing to do—come running after me.

But he didn't!

The night sky was incredibly dark, and the chilly air pierced my thin sweater. We didn't have a physical fight, but my bruised pride throbbed as I stomped up and down the streets in our neighborhood. I couldn't stay outside, yet I didn't want to go crawling back. Without a car or even my purse, what could I do?

Eventually there was no alternative. I *had* to

go home. In James 4:10 God promises that if we humble ourselves before the Lord, He will lift us up. I was feeling quite low at that point and I needed a little lifting. I knew I had to swallow my bruised pride and admit my own stubbornness to God and to my husband. It wasn't easy but I made myself do it. When I walked into the house I found Steve very loving, forgiving, and even a bit worried.

I knew the promise in James 4:10—in my head. I had even memorized it. But I remained very cold and lonely until I finally acted upon it and walked into the house. Until I humbled myself, there was no help—no change.

So the Lord has had to do a little work on me, teaching me to do some adjusting. But the hardest part of the learning process is when I *do* get my way and then can't enjoy it because I know I've manipulated my husband. He has only given in because he knows I'll make a fuss if I don't get what I want.

Frankly, I think marriage is the most beautiful and most difficult of all relationships. There's an old adage that says:

Needles and pins, needles and pins,
When a man marries his trouble begins.

Put two people who think they know everything about each other into a situation where they commit themselves to sharing the same home, food, dreams, and lifestyle, and they will soon discover how ignorant they are of one another. (A friend of mine was married three years before she found out her husband didn't like pepper on his eggs!)

Partners in every marriage have lived independently for twenty, thirty, sometimes forty years before they marry. They have grown up in different family backgrounds, lived on different schedules, been used to controlling their own lives. Suddenly everything is shared. In every decision each must consider the opinion and feelings of the other. They feel trapped.

When couples date they focus on how much they have in common. After marriage only the ways in which they are different seem important. Even in the most compatible marriages, honest couples admit there are days when they don't think they can stand each other one more minute. Anger feels quite at home.

Somehow, the expectations of a Cinderella/ Prince Charming, happily-ever-after marriage have so dominated our culture that whenever we encounter conflict or tension in marriage, we think we have made a mistake and are ready to tear up our marriage license.

The more divorce we see around us, the easier we accept it as an alternative. But many who have ended their marriages testify that divorce is not an escape; it's merely an exchange of one set of problems for another.

So, in the infinitely complex adjustments a married couple must make, is there really any hope? Are we doomed to a life of disappointments, angry fighting, and disagreement—or divorce?

No! There *is* hope when we plug into the rainbow of promises God has put in the Bible. Marriage was God's idea in the beginning. So if we have any questions about it, the best place to go is to Him. Genesis 2:24 says, "For this cause a man shall leave his father and his mother, and shall cleave to his wife; and they shall become one flesh" (NASB).

In our present American culture, we do fairly well at the "leaving" (of parents); it's the cleaving we have trouble with. The word cleave is a very strange one in today's English language. It has two directly opposite meanings. One is "to cut or split apart." The other is "to stick fast; adhere to; be faithful to." In the original language of the Old Testament those are two separate words. But the paradox in English is interesting. I think God would love to take many marriage relationships that have split apart and stick them back together.

The noun form for the Hebrew word "cleave" is the word for glue. I find that the more we as a couple stick together (like glue)—remain faithful to one another and simply show consideration for each other—the more we "become one." Genesis 2:24 is more than a platitude or a prophecy. It's a promise! They *shall* become one.

Faithfulness begins in the mind. Almost no one *intends* to become involved in an extramarital affair. But entertaining comparisons between my husband and someone else's, lingering over thoughts of the attractiveness of another, and allowing my mind to dwell on the impure conduct of others are sprouts of potential unfaithfulness.

One of the most vivid illustrations I saw of this was when I quit my job after we were married. I had nothing but time on my hands and nothing but soap operas to fill that time. The more I watched my "friends" on TV in their unhappy marriages, the more miserable I became in mine. Whenever my husband came home late I remembered the character in the soaps whose husband was unfaithful. I began to empathize with one woman who was unhappy because her husband didn't understand her needs. During each episode I found myself cheering her desperate attempt to get out of the marriage and justifying her search for love elsewhere.

When I realized what was happening to my own thought processes, I tried to quit watching. I couldn't believe how hooked I was. I tried to cut down, but the addiction was too strong. Finally, with the Lord's help, I had to quit "cold turkey." I decided that if I needed to be involved in other peoples' lives, there were plenty of hurting women around me who could use a friend. To this day, I can't watch one episode of a soap opera, even at a friend's house, or I find myself drawn into the web again.

For some of us, soap operas can erode our marital commitment quicker than anything else. There are enough subtle forces in this world to destroy our marriages, so it is especially important that we avoid such obvious ones as the daily soaps. To build up a marriage requires extra effort, but it's worth it.

I like the phrase "become one flesh" in the promise from Genesis because I see it as far more than the physical/sexual aspect of the marital union. We are becoming one in lifestyle, thoughts, desires, and all other areas of marriage. It's a process, though, not a Polaroid print.

The process of becoming one requires a close relationship, but it does not mean we have to smother our partners. We must keep a balance. We each need some privacy—some time alone to pursue the interests that make us individuals. Denying this "space factor" causes marital claustrophobia and chokes the life out of marriage.

As a couple we *must* grow. Unlike physical growth, however, growing a healthy relationship requires hard work. But a little fun can ease the growing pains.

Does the almighty God of the universe care about a struggling marriage? Yes! A thousand times, yes.

Several years ago, my husband and I became acquainted with a beautiful young woman—I'll call her Patty. Patty was the single parent of three small children. Her husband had been married previously, and his unreliability and chronic problem with chemical dependence made him a prime candidate for divorce number two. He got it.

But Patty's life began to change after the divorce. Someone told her that God loved her very much. The Creator of the world was so concerned about the problems and sin she had in her life that He sent His Son, the Lord Jesus Christ, to take them on Himself and die to pay the penalty for them. Patty trusted in Christ as her Savior, accepted His forgiveness for her sin, and asked Him to make her a new person—a Christian. He did.

As Patty studied the Bible, she believed God when He said He wanted marriage to be a once-for-all commitment. She plugged into the Genesis 2:24 promise.

Patty clung to the commitment she had made at her wedding ceremony and wouldn't give up. Over and over, in tears, she told us of her husband's broken promises to her and the children.

But God keeps *His* promises. As she prayed for His help and strength, He gave it. After several years of a very trying, roller-coaster relationship, her husband became a Christian. Some time later we were thrilled to attend a ceremony at which they renewed their vows.

Commitment is a rainbow of hope and promise.

If we take one of God's promises (like the one in Genesis 2:24) for our own, believe it, and step out in faith to act on what we believe, *that* is "plugging in" to God's power supply. The only condition is that we believe Him enough to act on His promise.

3 A Rainbow for a Mom Out of Control

Aside from a few early marriage spats, I didn't think I had much trouble with anger. As a matter of fact, I considered myself a fairly even-tempered person. Then I became a mother!

After my kids learned to talk, they learned to argue. There were times I thought I couldn't stand any more. Their "I did not," "You did too" battles would build until I couldn't be heard above them. I was trapped by the shouting syndrome. Many times I would find myself screaming to tell *them* to stop yelling.

Breakfast time has always brought out the worst in our kids. They can quarrel over anything.

"Mommy, nobody will get the cereal down for me. . . . Mommy, nobody will pour my milk for me."

"You didn't say please."

Someone throws a punch—it's returned by the recipient. Someone starts crying—loudly.

"Mommy, she finished up the Cheerios and I wanted some. I don't like puffed rice, and that's all that's left."

"I get the bike license plate from the cereal box."

"Oh, no you don't. You got the last one."

"Yeah, well that one got lost or bent up or something. I don't know what happened to it.

Besides, what would *you* use it for? You don't even have a bike."

"Why did I get the smallest piece of toast?"

"How come you got honey and I didn't?"

"Because that's all there was and you didn't get down here in time."

In tears, someone reaches across the table because someone else wouldn't pass the "whatever."

A spill.

By this time I am the one screaming and crying. How will I ever get soggy Cheerios out of shag carpeting? (Why do builders put shag carpeting in dining rooms, anyway?) Is there no end to quarreling and its devastating side effects?

But what makes me even more angry than quarreling is deliberate disobedience. Like the Irish father in Finian's Rainbow, there are times when I would say, "Give me strength to resist me own strength!" Perhaps it's just one more "hm—hm—hm—hm" after I've told my daughter to stop humming. Or maybe it's a major confrontation with my son about taking his bike out for a ride when he's grounded. But any alert parent can see that I-want-my-own-way nature in kids and will respond accordingly. Why is it that we use our gentlest words with friends and mere acquaintances and allow our harshest to fall on those we love most?

Little by little, the Lord has shown me that He has a special rainbow promise for me in this problem area too. A rainbow of gentleness and peace.

Gentleness and peace are the results of letting God's Spirit control our lives. Giving in to our natural responses, however, is much easier than allowing God to have control. "Thou wilt keep him in perfect peace whose mind is stayed on thee," God promises in Isaiah 26:3. So, I started trying to set my mind on Christ and to confess my anger. After all, according to God, uncontrolled anger is sin.

There are times, of course, when I let anger or another sin take over, but then I'm reminded of something else that's red—the blood of Christ that paid for every sin I've ever committed.

I was a child when I first realized the importance of Christ's death for my sin. Although I was outwardly fairly good, I knew what I was *really* like. As a child, I was one person in public and quite another at home. I remember my mother saying so many times, "Everybody thinks you're such a sweet little girl; if only they could see you now."

But there came a time when I took God seriously. I knew I had to make a decision to either accept His forgiveness or go my own way. In a simple prayer, I accepted the forgiveness He died to gain for me. He promises in His Word that "the blood of Jesus Christ his Son cleanses us from all sin" (1 John 1:7 NKJ). That's another promise! I took Him at His Word.

And the blood of Jesus Christ is as powerful to forgive today as it ever was—powerful enough to forgive even a mother's anger.

So I embarked on "project gentleness." The

Bible lists gentleness as a fruit of the Spirit, so its source must be the Spirit of God—God Himself. Since it wasn't something I could manufacture by myself, I began to pray specifically for this fruit to show up in my life. Anger and hostility only breed more of the same, so I couldn't help my children curb their anger with one another while my own was out of control.

I began learning how to yield myself to the Holy Spirit's control. But I wasn't an overnight success. God didn't zap me with automatic gentleness. It has been a step-by-step process— evaluating situations and trying to think before I speak (or yell).

It means asking for help from the Lord when I can't take any more (from a human standpoint). It means being willing to say I'm sorry and to ask my children's forgiveness (again) when I blow it and react in anger. It means keeping my mind on the Lord, who will give me the peace that rubs off on my children and others as gentleness.

One thing I learned from a very dear friend of mine is simply to watch the tone of my voice.

She and her husband give temporary care to children whose parents are in prison. The love that oozes from her in day-to-day conversations with those children is inspiring. It's amazing what a simple "honey" or "sweetheart" will do when it's added to even the most difficult parental requests.

I have begun to work on that with my own children. Sometimes I'll catch myself starting to yell or whine at them for their incessant arguing, and instead I'll be able to turn around everyone's whole attitude with a simple tone change and a "Please, honey?"

Of course, the best way to keep our minds "stayed on Him" is to study His Word every day. That is difficult when our children are small and we don't seem to have even five minutes to ourselves all day. But this promise is one of the conditional promises in Scripture. God's peace is ours *if* we keep our minds on Him. Christian books, radio, and records are helpful, but nothing can teach us more about Jesus and how He handled difficult situations than daily personal Bible study. To discover what God expects from us in our daily tasks, we need to read about God's dealings with people in Scripture and examine where they failed and where they succeeded.

Most important of all, I've noticed that the more time I spend with the Lord in prayer and meditating on His Word, the more His characteristics such as peace and gentleness (and the other fruit of the Spirit from Galatians 5:22–23) become my "natural reaction."

I don't have to stay out of control. I have His power and all of His resources available to me. Now I'm trying to use them.

Orange
Section

Protection

I know not where His islands lift
Their fronded palms in air;
I only know I cannot drift
Beyond His love and care.
                    —*John Greenleaf Whittier*

4 A Rainbow in the Maternity Ward

Perhaps the most severe test of my trust in God's promises came at the end of my second pregnancy. The crushing memory of an earlier miscarriage was still fresh. The fear of something going wrong hung over my husband and me like a thundercloud. As the due date loomed near, we were both eager for this child to be born.

The day our son decided to make his way into the world, I was preparing for a house guest, a missionary to New Guinea with whom I had corresponded for some time and who was to speak to our women's sewing group that weekend. The baby wasn't due for two weeks, so I invited her to stay with us. Besides, I was grateful for something else to think about.

As I rushed around the house straightening, vacuuming, and dusting—stooping, bending, and stretching—I began to feel what I later realized were labor pains. But they felt like little more than cramps, so I didn't worry about them. After all, I had two more weeks, didn't I?

We drove to the airport and picked up our guest. The sewing group met on the other side of town, nearly a 45-minute drive over some rather bumpy roads. They say that doesn't work, but I don't know . . . By the time we reached our destination I knew it would be a good idea to make arrangements for an alternate hostess. At ten o'clock that evening I checked into the maternity ward.

Fourteen *very* long hours later, our baby was born—a boy, just as we had dreamed! He was so sweet. I felt sure I had never seen tinier hands or fingernails or ears. The exhilaration of delivery created a high I never imagined. Everything was going perfectly!

No problem with a name for the little one. We had decided on that weeks before: Gregory—it sounded so strong—and Steven for a middle name (after his daddy, of course).

After a short visit with our tiny Gregory Steven Ellis, I returned to my room for a nap, and the new daddy, exhausted from staying up all night timing my contractions, went home for some sleep.

A short while later the pediatrician woke me. He was a short, stocky, brusque fellow whose "bedside manner" was totally non-existent! His news was not good, and he didn't clothe it with compassion. Something was wrong with our baby. He still didn't know the exact cause, but when the nurses had put little Greg in a warming bassinet, he had started to turn blue.

I swallowed hard. My former feelings of fear swelled to panic. Now what? I asked that someone phone my husband, but he didn't come. Waiting by myself added to my fright.

I later learned that when the nurse telephoned, Steve had barely dozed off. He answered the phone, but he was so exhausted he didn't understand her plea to return to the hospital. A second call finally registered, and he came as quickly as possible. His tender kiss reassured me that we were a team, trusting the Lord together for the outcome.

A specialist explained the baby's situation to us. Greg had a respiratory problem called Hyaline Membrane Disease (HMD), an immaturity in the lungs that keeps them from reinflating after they close. The condition is very rare in full-term babies, and they gave Greg about a 50/50 chance of survival. "I don't want to give you any false hope," the specialist said, "but if he makes it through the first 72 hours, he should be all right."

After signing a stack of papers to release Greg into the care of the staff at the University of Minnesota Hospital's Infant Intensive Care Unit, we watched blurry-eyed at the nursery window as they got him ready for the ambulance ride to a better-equipped hospital. Would I ever see little Greg again, alive? What was it like to pick out a casket for a baby? Had we waited so eagerly only to have our emotions dashed like the surf on a rugged shoreline?

The little blue card at the end of Greg's bassinet still read "Baby Ellis." I screamed inside. I had told them his name. Why hadn't they put it on the card as they had for the other babies in the nursery? Maybe they didn't want him to be a person yet in case he didn't make it. It seemed as if they had already signed his death certificate.

Back in my room after they took Greg away, I sent a question mark heavenward. *Not two babies, Lord,* I thought. *Please don't take two babies from me.*

Steve and I prayed together. "Lord, what does all this mean?" We made a few telephone calls, alerting friends and family to join us in prayer for the life of a very small person we already dearly loved.

Then in the quiet of my hospital room, Steve began reading to me from the Bible. He picked a portion at random—not generally a very wise practice, but logic is a stranger to crisis. "O Lord, thou hast searched me and known me. . . ." he read. The 139th Psalm said everything we needed to hear at that moment. The Lord had been in control of Steve's random selection. The personal God we loved and served knew every move we made. He had His hand on us. No matter how dark a situation we faced, He was with us, leading us by the hand. The specific rainbow promise we needed came in verse thirteen. "For thou has possessed my reins: *thou hast covered me in my mother's womb*" [italics mine].

Here was the assurance from God's living book that He had been watching over Greg all through my pregnancy. And the thought occurred to me, *Why should He stop now?*

We clung to that promise for each question and worry and fear. The following day the Sunday paper ran a feature story on HMD, educating us about our son's problem. As Steve and I read the article together, we felt sure God had placed it there for our benefit. Yet the statistics painted a frightening picture. HMD was the number one killer of newborn babies, taking 25,000 lives each year.

But God had given us His assurance, hadn't He? Could He be trusted? Twenty-five thousand babies a year . . . but not Greg? *Everyone* thinks it won't happen to *them.*

Perhaps the Lord would have given us a different verse if He had wanted to prepare us for Greg's death. We hung on tightly to the promise He gave, trusting that if Greg wasn't going to make it, the Lord would prepare us for that as well.

For several days I didn't see Greg. I had to finish my "sentence" in the maternity ward. The hospital became my prison while my baby lay in an incubator miles away. He needed me, didn't he? I cried in the morning when I woke. My arms ached each time my roommate nursed her tiny one. Sad? Yes! But I was surprised at the absence of bitterness or depression. I tried to direct my questions to the Lord, and He took care of the emotions.

I kept in touch with the University Hospital staff several times daily by phone. They encouraged me to call even in the middle of the night if I was concerned and wanted to know how Greg was doing.

Steve relayed reports of how pitiful our baby looked in the incubator. But even with his warnings, I wasn't prepared for what I saw when I was finally able to visit.

There he lay, his little chest sunken in, fighting

for every breath. Pure oxygen was being pumped into him through a large plastic bubble over his head. They had been trying for days to reduce the percentage of oxygen, but each time it would have to be raised again to ease his breathing. Circles of gauze covered his eyes (held in place by a narrow elastic bandage) to protect them from the special lights that would correct the jaundice he had developed.

As I looked at that pathetic little body laced with tubes and monitor leads, it was difficult to believe that God knew what He was doing. Our baby could hardly move or cry. It took all of his strength just to breathe. But we *had* to trust the Lord. We *had* to lean on Him. And the more we leaned, the stronger we became.

Our trust in the Lord wasn't something we grasped for in a crisis situation. It was a steady leaning on the relationship we had already developed with Jesus Christ.

And so, eleven days after that dreadful conversation with the pediatrician, we took Greg home. His jaundice was gone, his blood fine, and his lungs clear and functioning beautifully on their own. In fact, can you imagine new parents cheering when their baby lets out a lusty cry? We did. The doctors said crying was good for him. It strengthened his lungs. (I must admit, however, that our enthusiasm for his crying did begin to wear off after a few days.)

Since Greg's bout with HMD (now better known as RDS—Respiratory Distress Syndrome) new techniques and treatments have lowered the mortality rate drastically. But during that time of crisis for us, we knew those doctors had divine assistance in caring for a special little boy.

As we yielded our "rights" to a baby of our own and trusted the God who promised to watch over that baby, God Himself strengthened our relationship with Him.

5 A Rainbow for Babies and Drugs

As our family grew, so did our relationship with the Lord. One day after another crisis situation— this time with our third child—our pastor told us that couples without children probably never learn what it means to trust the Lord in the same way parents do. We were learning what he meant.

The spring and summer of 1977 were rough for my parents. My dad had been out of work for several months when my mother suffered a stroke. At first she was completely paralyzed on one side, but she improved at an encouraging rate.

When she came home from the hospital Dad still had no work. He tried to keep up with the housecleaning and dishes, but his constant job-hunting left little time for domestic chores. Mom grew depressed and frustrated at the mounting work and her inability to do anything.

A teary phone call from her one morning spurred me into action. I fed the kids an early lunch and made a cold supper to eat when we returned. It was one of those hot summer days when a salad would taste great, anyway. I packed up our three kids (ages six, four, and eighteen months) and drove the short distance.

Dad let me in, then left quickly for a job interview. I took Maryanne, our youngest, upstairs to Mom and Dad's room and laid her in a playpen, carefully pulling the playpen away from Mom's dresser. I covered Maryanne with her favorite blanket. She looked as if she could fall asleep any minute. I assumed she would. She still took long naps—sometimes for two or three hours.

Downstairs, I gave the other two children some toys and books to keep them occupied. Grandma appreciated having the children near her. Then, kicking off my sandals, I went to work.

When Dad came home a couple hours later, he went upstairs to see if Maryanne was awake.

I was finishing my last chore, mopping the kitchen floor, when Dad brought Maryanne downstairs and set her on the carpeting. I peeked through the doorway just in time to see her totter, then fall down.

"Honey, she's not quite awake yet," Mom said to Dad.

When Maryanne struggled to get up she looked like a buoy bobbing in the lake. She couldn't seem to right herself.

Not knowing anything was wrong, six-year-old Greg laughed at his little sister. "Look at silly Maryanne," he said. He thought she was playing.

When I walked over to her she tried to talk, but a high, sing-songy voice came out. I picked her up and looked at her eyes. They looked strange and glassy. My heart started pounding. I didn't know what was wrong.

Then Dad came downstairs again—this time with an empty pill bottle and a couple of Valium tablets in his hand. I'll never forget the look on his face as he told me that the playpen was up against Mom's dresser. He had found the pill bottle in the playpen and the Valium on the floor.

Holding the baby tightly, I slipped into my sandals and headed for the car. "I'd better get her to Children's Hospital right away," I called over my shoulder. I glanced at my watch. "Steve should be home any minute . . ."

"I'll pick him up and meet you there," Dad said. "You go ahead."

As I drove to the hospital clutching Maryanne close to me, she chattered in that strange voice. Tears filled my eyes as I prayed for God's guidance and help. My stomach burned with fear and unbelief. I was so careful, yet it happened anyway!

When Dad and Steve joined me in the emergency room Dad had more bad news. Maryanne had gotten into Mom's Digitalis as well as the Valium. He brought the bottles so the doctors would know what they were dealing with. Still we didn't know how much she had ingested.

The nurses gave Maryanne some syrup of Ipecac to induce vomiting. As I took her sunsuit off, I noticed small red rings on her back. I asked Dad for one of the pill container lids. The circles and lids matched. Apparently she had gotten into the medications *before* she fell asleep, so the drugs were well into her system. The Ipecac wouldn't help.

Dad went home to help Mom take care of our

other two children, and the hospital staff put Maryanne in a ward where they could observe her. There wasn't much else they could do.

I spent six long hours holding and rocking her. She wouldn't settle down. She was hysterical. The heart monitors attached to her chest bothered her. She kept trying to pull them off.

Evidently, the drugs began giving her some weird sensations. When I started reading a book to her, she quieted down for a few minutes, then let out a scream, violently pushing the book away as though she thought something were trying to attack her.

Sometimes Steve would hold her for a while, but most of the time Maryanne wanted Mommy. And that was unusual for this child who had always been "Daddy's girl!"

Just when I finally got her to sleep, the nurse had to take more blood samples. Maryanne woke up again, screaming, and it took another couple of hours for her to fall asleep for the night.

Steve decided to go pick up our other two children and get them into their own beds. "Will you be all right?" he asked.

"Sure," I said. But I *wasn't* sure. I worried about what long-term effects this could have on our little daughter.

Once again, though, what *I* couldn't do, the Lord could and did. During those hospital hours another of God's promises gained new meaning for me. "The eternal God is your refuge, and underneath are the everlasting arms" (Deuteronomy 33:27).

Those arms of His love were under me and all around me that night. There wasn't anything I could do for my baby. The drugs had to run their course. All I could do was be there and pray. Others were praying too. And I knew that God was there.

The nurses provided a make-shift bed for me in a nearby waiting room. It wasn't very comfortable, but I dozed.

Once again the Lord had to bring me to a place of absolute helplessness to show me I *could* trust His promises.

When we're wrestling with our own personal problems we often feel as if we can trust the Lord and still have a hand in what happens. But parents feel so helpless watching their children go through the agonies they must face. We want to jump in and spare them, make it easier, help them escape the pain. But we can't always do that. And so, as we stand by and watch, we learn to let God's rainbow of protection curl around us and our children. We can trust Him for the outcome.

Sometimes the waiting seems unbearable. Although Maryanne was discharged the next afternoon, it took time for the effects of those drugs to wear off. For three days she spoke in that high, sing-songy voice and tottered as she walked. Yet as far as we knew there was no lasting heart or brain damage.

But even if there had been, would that have nullified God's promises to us? No! He never asks us to endure anything more than we can stand. We can trust Him to always do what's best because *God is God*. It would be totally against His character to do anything that isn't ultimately in our best interest.

No matter what the storm is like we can come to the Lord for refuge, shelter, and protection. He'll never turn us away. Underneath are the solid, loving, everlasting arms.

Yellow
Section

Fear

To him who is in fear everything rustles.
　　　　　　　　　　　　　　—*Sophocles*

A Rainbow for Superwoman

Some rainbows come in the crises, but others come in the "ordinary."

I am a rather curious combination of Superwoman and the Cowardly Lion. One part of me thinks I can do everything; the other part is afraid to do anything.

Often when I plan a big dinner party, I resolve to do everything myself. I cook, clean, set the table with its finery, and try to keep the kids out of the dessert. By the time our guests arrive I am a nervous wreck. Yet if someone would offer to help in the kitchen I would shoo them out quickly, insisting that everything was under control.

A few years ago, I tried working four or five evenings a week, keeping up with my church responsibilities, and maintaining a smooth-functioning home with three young children. I wound up in bed for six weeks!

I know I'm not alone in this "superwoman" mentality.

A certain perfume commercial on TV reinforces our conviction that we should *all* be able to live the life of Superwoman. A professional-looking woman appears on the screen twirling her belt while singing a song about how she can bring home the bacon *and* cook it. Then, letting her hair down and striking a provocative pose, she asserts that she is also capable of never letting "him" forget he's a man.

That commercial bothers me. It reflects society's unfair pressure to mold us into superwomen. "If a woman can't hold down a '9 to 5,' do her own cooking and cleaning, and still keep her 'man' happy sexually, she's a failure," says this philosophy. Add a few children and Superwoman has to be quite a gal!

Frankly, I have problems with the superwoman mind-set—and not only in the area of working. That way of thinking has gotten me into trouble all too often. In fact, it is what brought about my miscarriage.

Less than a year after we were married, we moved into a lovely old three-bedroom house with a fireplace—a dream! About the same time we learned the delightful news that we would have our first child in about seven months. I could hardly contain my excitement!

From my "Cinderella and the Prince" outlook, I wondered what could be more perfect. We were both elated.

But as the June sun beat down on the white stucco exterior of our first house, the interior began to feel like an oven. "I've got to get the screens up," I told myself. "Steve will be tired when he gets home from work. I'm sure I can handle it myself." The unpacking was almost done, and the new curtains I had made already hung at the windows.

Feeling independent, I went out to the garage to figure out which screens fit which windows. I leaned a couple of screens against the house and began the task of taking down the storm windows.

When I realized how heavy they were, I hesitated a moment—my mother had warned me about doing any heavy lifting or moving during my first few weeks of pregnancy, but I dismissed the thought. *I'm strong and healthy,* I thought. *I'll be OK.*

I finished in little more than an hour.

Within a few days, though, I lay in bed. All I could do was wait and see if the baby would make it, my obstetrician told me. Meanwhile, I had to stay off my feet completely. My Prince waited on his Cinderella hand and foot and tried to cook light meals as the doctor suggested.

But the hemorrhaging worsened, and soon I was in the hospital. Tests confirmed my fears. I had lost the baby.

There was something about the antiseptic atmosphere of the hospital that seemed to bounce my grief off the walls and echo sorrow all over the room. I was crushed. A part of me died that day.

I had a lovely roommate and an assortment of visitors, but I felt very much alone.

"The Lord has a reason for this," everyone said in one way or another.

"No!" I wanted to shout. "It's all *my* fault. I wanted the baby so much, yet through my own arrogance . . . " I started to say I killed it, but that was too hard. One minute I blamed myself and the next minute I blamed God.

I somehow managed to appear calm and say all the right words of acceptance, but inwardly I fumed. *Some women don't want their babies,* I shouted silently. *I wanted mine and God took it away. It's not fair!* I had learned, however, that I could lean on Christ in difficult circumstances, so I tried. I prayed. I begged for inner peace. But it took time—time for me to learn that God is not my puppet, dancing to the tune I pipe; time for me to learn that I was not strong—without Him; time to prepare, to learn to feel deeply with other women I would meet who had also lost babies *they* really wanted.

Maybe it was time to see a new rainbow from God's Word.

During my recuperation at home, an unmarried friend brought me a gift. Having mastered the art of calligraphy, she lettered Ecclesiastes 3:11 in flowery script on a gold-edged piece of stationery. A few small stalks of grain set off the simple words of that verse: "He hath made every thing beautiful *in His time*" (KJV, italics mine).

She said a few words before leaving me to my thoughts, but I don't remember what they were—I just remember my surprise at her sensitivity and thoughtfulness. I didn't know she could understand.

For a while her special letter sat in a drawer as a keepsake. Then one day I took my treasure from its hiding place, mounted it on a dark piece of wood, and hung it on the wall. Now it's a constant reminder that God's timing is not always ours.

As a result of that experience I *began* to understand my "limits," but another threatening situation persuaded me to take a closer look at the superwoman mentality.

The winter's first accumulation of snow had fallen, and I was one of the first drivers on the newly plowed freeway as I drove to a meeting early one crisp Saturday morning. My husband had warned me to be careful because the roads might be slippery, and I assured him I would be. As usual, though, I got started a little late, so I drove a bit faster to compensate for my delays.

The roads were clear, and I laughed quietly at my husband's caution. *I'm a good driver,* I thought. *I can handle things.*

Then I drove under an overpass.

Suddenly the car spun out of control. I whipped the steering wheel around, but it did no good. Snow smothered the windshield and windows. I couldn't see! The car spun still more before coming to a stop after the motor died.

But where was I? The wipers wouldn't work. Shaking, I tried the ignition. No power. On which side of the median had the car stopped? I was afraid to get out. I could be hit. But I couldn't sit there!

"Dear Lord, I've got to know where I am. Please don't let anyone hit me." Finally I had the presence of mind to roll down the window and look out.

The Lord is good. The car had only spun off the road and up the embankment, but it was headed the wrong direction. Alone and fright-

ened, I prayed again. "Lord, what do I do now?"
I was already late for an important meeting, and
people were waiting for me. I knew I must be
quite a distance from a phone. I've heard you
should stay with your car after an accident, but
there was very little traffic. The choice was risky,
but I decided I had to get out and walk if I
wanted any help.

That's when another familiar verse became a
rainbow of promise, as well as rebuke, for me.
"I can do *all* things . . . " But how? Superwoman had forgotten to include the how . . .
"*through Christ* who strengthens me" (Philippians 4:13 NKJ). God did say I could do all things,
but He said it was through Christ—in relying on
His power—that I could do it. I am not *self*-
sufficient! Jesus said, "Without Me you can do
nothing" (John 15:5 NKJ). Although negative,
that's a kind of promise too. But He also
promises that His strength is made perfect in
weakness (2 Corinthians 12:9 NKJ).

As I trusted in Him for my strength and started
walking bootless through the deep snow toward
the next exit, the Lord sent *His* answer to my
prayer. Within minutes a station wagon stopped,
and a nice-looking woman asked me if I wanted
a ride. I hesitated, feeling a bit cautious, but
finally agreed.

Riding in her warm, comfortable car, we talked
about the accident. Gradually I realized that the
music on her car radio was from a local Christian
station. Through our conversation I discovered
that my rescuer was a Christian too. The Lord

had sent one of His own to see that I arrived safely at a place where I could get some help.

After that incident I learned how important it is to "know my limits." Just as I had exceeded the speed limit on that snowy morning, I was also habitually exceeding my health limits, mental and emotional limits, and even service limits. I asked my husband to help me assess how much I could do without breaking the laws of my own body, mind, and spirit.

Steve now helps me plan my schedule. I check with him for advice before making any major commitments. He encourages me to say no if a particular speaking trip or time commitment will tax my strength beyond reasonable limits. This frees me from the guilt I might feel as a result of turning someone down. I'm benefiting from his more objective viewpoint.

He has the freedom to say "Please listen to me," since he can be more objective. He *does* receive wisdom from God, and I'm learning to trust his judgment. My husband isn't trying to cramp my style when he asks certain things of me or cautions me about other things. He really cares.

God can work through our husbands to help us make the best decisions; to maintain a balanced, sensible schedule; and to avoid a health breakdown.

God never asked me or anyone else to be a superwoman. Superwoman is a fictional character! Society conjured her up, and only pride pressures us to live up to her image.

When I let God take charge, He constantly surprises me with His tremendous power. He gives me the strength to *do* and *be* whatever He asks of me if I put myself in His hands and quit trying to run the show.

7 A Rainbow for the Cowardly Lion

The superwoman pursuit is sometimes a way of handling fear—the fear of failing society's standards. But there is also another kind of personal fear that plagues me from time to time.

The Cowardly Lion (also known as superchicken) part of me is sometimes paralyzed by fear. I get terrified at the very thought of going to the dentist. Or hand me a list of ten people and suggest that I ask them to each bring three dozen cookies for an afternoon tea and I'll freeze. I can speak before an audience of hundreds of people with relative ease (if I'm prepared), but suggest that I go next door and introduce myself to my new neighbor and I'm petrified.

The older I get, the more my fears seem to increase. Things I never used to think twice about now make me afraid. I remember clopping across suspension foot bridges without a thought of danger. But on a recent vacation, I clung to a tree on the "safe side" while the rest of my family enjoyed the swinging bridge and the view from the other side.

I used to have no fear of height. As a young teen, I ascended the stairs of many state capitol buildings during family vacations and enjoyed the view from the top. But a few years ago, I tried climbing the lookout tower at Lake Itasca State Park in Minnesota. The wind began to blow, the tower began to sway, and the steps felt very shaky beneath me. I looked straight down and panicked! Although I was only about a third of the way up the tower, I couldn't go on. Our three children, accompanied by their father, waved to me from the top. They were disappointed in me, but I couldn't go any higher.

Perhaps the fear that twists my stomach most often is the fear of getting lost. When I started traveling to unfamiliar places for speaking engagements I grew to appreciate my husband's profession. Steve works for the Department of Transportation, so he knows the state roadways well. I, on the other hand, have a terrible sense of direction. If there is any possibility of making a wrong turn or missing an exit or getting the directions mixed up in any way, I will do it. I have gotten to the point that I celebrate when I reach my destination *without* any unplanned side-trips.

I remember one incident in particular. I was following my directions carefully but couldn't find the right town. I hadn't made any wrong turns that I knew of. I kept driving and driving, but no town of that name seemed to exist. The time of my expected arrival drew closer, and I prayed desperately. "Lord, please help me. Have I missed a turn or somehow passed this place without knowing it? Please help."

His little rainbow promise came that day in the form of a song based on Scripture. It was a song our church choir had been rehearsing for several weeks as we prepared to sing Mendelssohn's oratorio *Elijah*. " 'Be not afraid,' saith God the Lord. 'Be not afraid, thy help is near, for He is near.' " Those words are repeated over and over and the music builds in intensity until we *have* to believe it.

I knew many instances in the Bible where the Lord said "Be not afraid." I knew the promise of Psalm 46:1–2: "God is our refuge and strength, an ever present help in trouble. Therefore we will not fear. . . ."

I took God at His Word and kept driving, singing the song over and over out loud. Within minutes I saw the building I was looking for and rejoiced that God had once again quieted my fears. I really *could* trust Him!

During a period of time a few years ago, a different kind of fear held me in its grip longer than I'd like to admit.

When I was in high school, my very godly grandfather died, and Grandma came to live with us. We bought a big, two-story house that provided separate living quarters for her. My mother was working then, and on many cold, wintry afternoons when I came home from school, Grandma would be waiting for me with a pot of hot tea on her stove.

I would sit in her cozy little kitchen and pour out all that happened during the day, and she would listen. We would talk about what the Lord was teaching both of us in our very different walks with Him. Those were beautiful times together.

Then Grandma married an older bachelor who had loved her from afar when they were both in their teens. They moved to the outer suburbs, and my grandma and I grew apart a little.

Not long after that my parents moved our family from St. Louis, Missouri, to Minneapolis, Minnesota, so Dad could find work. Grandma and I grew a little further apart.

Still there was something special between Grandma and me every time we went home for a visit. When she developed severe health problems we began to pray that the Lord would mercifully take her home to end her suffering.

He answered our prayers.

I praised the Lord for His answer when we received the news, but it really hadn't sunk in that Grandma was gone. I didn't even cry until the funeral. Then all the wonderful things she had done through the years to further the cause of Christ were enumerated. Most people never knew about those things. Even I didn't know many of them. I broke down—not out of sorrow for her but out of the realization that her service was done. I wondered if anyone could fill her shoes. I cried because I couldn't sit and talk with her or enjoy a cup of tea with her or learn how to be a woman of God from her anymore.

I wondered what could be said of me at my funeral. What of eternal value was I doing with my life? For the first time I dealt with my own mortality. For months I struggled with an uncanny fear—the fear of death and of what was beyond.

The Bible teaches that all who trust Christ's death and resurrection (and that alone) to take away their sins can be sure they will go to heaven. I had done that. But I was terrorized by such questions as How will it happen? Will it be painful? What will it be like? Can I really believe everything the Bible says about death?

It was a long-lasting, nagging fear—a struggle to really believe God was totally in control.

Perhaps my mother's illness at the time also nagged at me from the corners of my mind. Her recent stroke and her bout with breast cancer a few years before remained fresh in my memory. I also knew that when my dad was a teenager, his mother had died of breast cancer. With the heredity factor lurking on both sides of the family, my mind became more than a little preoccupied with "the odds."

I thought back to the first time I had been near someone who died. Our family was at a week-end Bible conference far from home. After the Sunday morning worship service, when we were about to leave, one of the preachers slipped down from his chair onto the floor.

Although I was only ten or eleven years old, I clearly remember watching a nurse try to revive him. But he was dead. Yet not really, I told myself at the funeral home. He never actually ceased to be alive. He simply changed residences—from earth to heaven.

After my grandmother died I struggled for some time with my unanswered questions. Again the breakthrough came for me from a song—this time a contemporary gospel song by Don Wyrtzen entitled *Finally Home*. The chorus says:

But just think of stepping on shore, and finding it
    heaven:
Of touching a hand and finding it God's,
Of breathing new air and finding it celestial,
Of waking up in Glory, and finding it *home!*

That song led me into the Scriptures. "Let not
your heart be troubled: ye believe in God,
believe also in me. In my Father's house are
many mansions: if it were not so, I would have
told you. I go to prepare a place for you. . . . I
will come again, and receive you unto myself;
that where I am, there ye may be also" (John
14:1–3 KJV). Although I had memorized this
passage as a child, I found it now had new
meaning. The song made the promise extremely
personal, and the Scripture made it completely
trustworthy!

God's presence is with me through all sorts of
fears. He quiets those fears no matter how silly
they may seem to others. And the fear of
death—the ultimate fear (because it's the ultimate enemy)—began to dissolve as I trusted His
promise.

Green
Section

Selfishness

Selfishness is not living as one wishes to live; it is asking others to live as one wishes to live.

—*Oscar Wilde*

8 A Rainbow for #1

My problem with selfishness began long before I was married. My most painful experience with it happened the summer I graduated from high school. Our family moved 600 miles only six days after my graduation. Three weeks after that, and before we had even found a home, I flew (by myself) to Central America to work with a missionary family for two and a half months.

I loved the excitement, independence, and feeling of accomplishment. But even though I had been away from home many times before, the culture shock and separation of so many miles germinated into a severe case of home-sickness.

As the time for my return approached, I became more and more excited. I was scheduled to arrive home on my birthday, and I knew Mom would make it special. Also, throughout the summer I had corresponded with a very good friend, and I was anxious to see *him* again.

As my friend drove me home from the airport, I looked forward to being the center of attention for a while. After all, I had "done without" so many things over the summer that I deserved a little special treatment, didn't I?

When I walked in the front door of our new house I was greeted by relatives and young people from our new church. My mother had arranged a surprise birthday party for me. Thrilling, right? Except the biggest surprise was that I wasn't the only guest of honor! While my mother was inviting people to a surprise party for me, the sister-in-law of a certain single fellow named Steve (whom I viewed as a stick-in-the-mud) was inviting the same people to a birthday party for him. Since our birthdays were the same day they decided to combine the parties and invite everyone to our house. As a surprise, the party was a success! At sharing the spotlight, I was a failure!

By staying close to my date, I managed to enjoy the party. After all, I *was* glad to be home. And little did I know then that someday I would not only be sharing birthdays with Steve but his last name, his home, his car, and a marriage license as well.

Sharing his name, home, and car didn't bother me much. I rather liked the idea since the inevitable had happened. I had fallen in love with this man I discovered wasn't a stick-in-the-mud after all. But the birthday—that was another story. To make matters worse—it didn't seem to bother *him*. He thought it was great!

As I was growing up, birthdays were very special. The birthday child was "the star" all day long. He or she could decide what the family would have for dinner that night (within reason), often went shopping alone with Mom for a new outfit of clothes, never was required to do the dishes after dinner, and generally had the place of preeminence for that day.

How in the world can you share stardom?

When Steve and I got married I felt I should

make his birthday special—bake a cake just for him, take him out to dinner, buy him a nice gift. But it was *my* birthday too. That meant I was deprived of one dinner out *every* year.

Immaturity? Yes. That's what selfishness is.

Today all kinds of books encourage soloing, a form of selfishness. Authors have told us how to look out for number one, pull our own strings, and say no without feeling guilty. Some of us may need to be a bit more assertive, but a bigger need is to be less self-centered. When one person insists on singing a solo, unaccompanied, the music has no harmony. And personal relationships become dissonant in contests of who's number one. On the occasions that marital tension has cropped up between my husband and me, its roots have been in selfishness. I want my husband to fulfill my needs and supply all my wants. I expect him to know automatically what is upsetting me. Sometimes, of course, that doesn't take much.

A few years ago I read a book that encouraged each Christian woman to keep her home and personal appearance so attractive that her husband would relish coming home. I felt convicted and spent half of one whole day straightening and cleaning. The other half I used for showering, curling my hair, and fixing Steve's favorite meal. For the finishing touch I even wore an outfit he especially liked. (All of this while trying to keep my three preschoolers from killing each other.)

When my husband arrived, he didn't seem to

notice my efforts. I moped around, pouting and closing cupboard doors a bit more noisily than necessary. Eventually he asked what was wrong.

"If you don't know, I'm not going to tell you," I replied in classic fashion.

Later, after the air finally cleared, I found out he *had* noticed. He simply hadn't realized how important it was to me for him to *say* so.

We have played similar scenes far too many times.

Recently our pastor said something that helped me see the real problem. In a message on the wife's responsibilities in marriage he tried to give the man's viewpoint. "We men cannot do it alone," he said. "We're unsure of ourselves. We don't know how to love you as we ought to love you. We need instruction. We need guidance. We need help. And although many times we would rather not let on, the fact is that we worry about giving to our marriage the strength that it needs. We want to do what's right. We really do. We want to be strong. We want to be leaders. But we can't do it alone. We need you. Our success depends on you. So please don't compete with us. Don't make it more difficult than it already is. Give us all the help you possibly can."

Suddenly I understood. I *had* been competing with Steve—pushing for my own way instead of letting him lead. I *had* been making it more difficult. I had been expecting him to be a mind reader—to know what I expected of him in everything from romance to household duties.

Yet we hadn't spent much time at all discussing those matters.

The rainbow of promise for both these problems is found in a verse I had memorized before I went to Central America. "I will never leave thee, nor forsake thee" (Hebrews 13:5 KJV). That was a wonderful promise for a seventeen-year-old girl traveling 2500 miles to live with a family she had never seen before. But the remainder of the verse is particularly appropriate for the problem of selfishness. The New International Version puts it this way: "Keep your lives free from the love of money and be content with what you have, because God has said, 'Never will I leave you; *never* will I forsake you' " [italics mine].

Suddenly I realized that this promise was given in the context of covetousness—wanting what we don't have or not being content with what we do have. Wanting all the attention, both from my friends as a teenager and from Steve as his wife, was selfish. And now, in addition, I realized that covetousness was creeping into my life as a young housewife. I had begun to crave nice things. I didn't *always* find the Lord to be enough.

I needed that rainbow: *Be content with Me; I am always with you.*

"But Lord," I argued, "I have the worst-looking sofa in the whole neighborhood. I know—I've been to every house and checked. Everybody else's is at least two years newer than mine."

"Be content with Me," Jesus says.

"But, Lord, I really could use a new dress. There are only so many ways you can wear two skirts and three blouses."

"Be content with Me."

"But Lord, what about when I haven't been out alone with my husband for over two months—or is it three?"

"Be content with Me."

"Lord, what about when the *other* author's books get more promotion than mine?"

"Be content with Me. I'm in control."

His patience is amazing!

Regardless of what form selfishness takes—coveting things, wanting my needs met, or being too ambitious—it can evaporate when I relax in the contentment of knowing the Lord Jesus Christ and trusting Him. He is the divine need-meeter (our husbands were never meant to be). He knows our needs far better than we do.

If we spend all our time trying to get others to meet our needs, we won't have time to *do* anything for the Lord.

Calvary Free Church
P.O. Box 358
Walker, MN 56484

9 A Rainbow for Envy

After working with a small, inner-city church for more than seven years, my husband and I began attending a much larger church. Our previous church had no choir. On rare occasions when they needed special music they usually asked me to sing. I loved music, and I was looking forward to participating in the music ministry at our new church and the opportunities for creative expression that it would provide.

There were some excellent musicians in the choir, and most of them regarded their music as a ministry, not a performance. I liked that. However, I was not prepared for any competition.

A few months after I joined the choir at our new church home, we began preparing a cantata for the fall missions conference. Our director asked me to sing one of the solos. I appreciated the opportunity to convey a challenging message through a lovely melody and enjoyed the fulfillment it gave me as well.

When we began working on the Christmas cantata, I waited to see which solo would be mine, but I was not given one. Another young woman, whom I'll call Colleen, was given one of the soprano solos, and a *tenor* was given the other! Colleen had already started working on a solo verse for a choir anthem we would sing the week before Christmas. I simmered with selfishness and jealousy. Why should Colleen get both solos? How could the choir director be so unfair?

How could *I* be so petty? Yet it hurt.

One night my jealousy surfaced bitterly. I don't know how long I lay crying on my bed, but I felt very foolish. Such a childish reaction! I hated myself for my attitude, but I couldn't seem to change it.

Steve sat beside me, running his fingers through my hair and trying to comfort me. He said all the things I had already told myself: The Lord must have wanted Colleen to have the solo. He is sovereign and makes no mistakes. There's something He must want me to learn from all of this.

I tried to think of my feelings as sin and to ask forgiveness, but I rebelled. I was wounded.

But the Lord kept after me. He reminded me of His principle of going to one another in love. "Confess your sins to each other and pray for each other so that you may be healed," James 5:16 says. I knew I needed Colleen's forgiveness as well as the Lord's.

Finally I claimed God's promise in 1 John 1:9: "If we confess our sins, He is faithful and just and will forgive us our sins and purify us from all unrighteousness." I knew God had forgiven me, but until I talked to Colleen I wouldn't feel right. And talking to her wouldn't be easy.

It would have been simpler if her voice was inferior to mine. Then asking her forgiveness could have been a gesture of condescension. But

I admired Colleen. She was a beautiful Christian with a lovely voice. It was hard to bridle my pride.

Several weeks went by, and the "cowardly lion" within me delayed talking to her about it. Then one night after choir rehearsal, when I had almost mustered the courage to say something to her, she stopped me in the hall. I wasn't prepared for what she had to say.

"Joyce, I can't keep it in any longer," she began. "I have to ask your forgiveness for something."

I frowned in confusion. What could Colleen need my forgiveness for?

She proceeded to tell me how she had felt threatened when I joined the choir. She felt I was getting some of the choice solos, including the one she had hoped for in the missionary cantata.

I couldn't believe it. Colleen was struggling with the same conflict that plagued me.

"The Lord has had to deal harshly with me for my attitude," she continued. "What difference does it make which vessel He uses to bless His people, as long as they're blessed? And Joyce, I know He is using you to bless people. You've blessed me with your music, and I want you to forgive me for being jealous of you."

My cheeks burned. Both of us had tears in our eyes. It was hard for me to counter with my own confession. Somehow the words tumbled out. "Oh, Colleen, I've been so jealous of you and your two solos at Christmas. I feel so stupid! Can you forgive me?"

We were like a couple of little girls making up on the school playground, but what a difference it made. I realized that I had been so bound by my jealousy that I hadn't been free to receive the blessing the Lord wanted me to have through *her* music.

I can't bear to think of what might have happened to the whole choir's ministry if we hadn't rooted out those poisonous feelings toward one another.

The Lord sometimes uses our weaknesses to transform us into the people He wants us to become. Now a special friendship exists between Colleen and me because the Lord exposed our faults and we dealt with them. Now we pray for one another and the ministries the Lord has given each of us.

The seeds of jealousy still crop up sometimes, but I have found another rainbow promise since that incident that has really helped.

In 1 Corinthians 3:3 the apostle Paul talks about the jealousy that existed in the church at Corinth. He says, "Since there is jealousy and quarreling among you, are you not worldly?"

Me? Worldy? Paul, you don't understand!

In verse five he continues, "What, after all, is Apollos? And what is Paul?" (He might as well have said, "What is Colleen? What is Joyce?") "Only servants . . . as the Lord has assigned to each his task."

In some ways the dispute in Corinth was different. Their jealousy caused them to feel superior to one another, but it was also causing them to become very sectarian. They may have said such things as "You know, Paul himself led *me* to the Lord." Another might have responded, "Well, I can't help it that Paul didn't come to my town, but Apollos is the newest preacher around, and he was the one who showed me the way to become a Christian."

In other ways our conflict was very much the same. Jealousy and envy, in whatever form they take, hurt deeply.

Paul goes on to say that while some serve one function and others serve another, only God can bring about growth and blessing. Then comes the promise: "Each will be rewarded according to his own labor" (v. 8).

As Colleen said, "It doesn't matter whom God uses to bless His people." God will take care of the results and reward us for our efforts if we are faithful and use our gifts for *His* glory, not ours.

So when jealousy creeps in, whether it's with Colleen or someone else, I try to smile and pray for that person. I pray that the Lord will be magnified through his or her talent and that people will be blessed.

Blue
Section

Coldness

Cold the stars are, cold the earth is,
Everything is grim and cold!

—*William Winter*

10 A Rainbow for the Common Cold-ness

Earlier, I alluded to a time when I tried to work evenings and keep everything together at home. That was one of the most difficult times of my life.

When we started our family Steve and I agreed that I would not take an outside job as long as our children were small. But when a severe financial crunch hit our budget, I offered to get a job in the evenings so Daddy could be home with the kids. Steve reluctantly agreed, and I contacted a woman from a needlecraft company who wanted me to be an instructor for their home party plan.

At each party, the instructor would teach two or three new crafts and then sell kits to the guests. I enjoy all sorts of needlework, so I was a natural for the job. This seemed like the perfect solution.

I breezed through the training and began to get excited about the earning possibilities. After I started to book parties, my calendar looked like a heavy novel—no white space. Occasionally I questioned the pace, but Superwoman was not dead. *I can handle it,* I thought.

Two problem areas became immediately apparent, however. Trying to follow directions to the party location was the first one. I got lost and made wrong turns so many times I lost count! Occasionally I arrived late for the party, causing my hostess to bite her nails and wonder what she was going to do with thirty-seven bored women in her living room.

Math was my second problem area. It had never been one of my academic strengths, and I soon learned that my abilities had not improved with time. Many weeks I spent more time trying to get the figures to agree than actually teaching and selling. And my husband remembers all the times my checkbook wouldn't balance!

In time, the math became less troublesome, but it was replaced by other problems. I had a lot of bookings, but the profits other instructors earned from their parties still eluded me. I determined to work harder.

I also had to complete samples of all the projects so my customers could see how they looked when they were finished. I spent most of my days and occasional free evenings watching television and working on needlepoint, latch-hook, and crewel. Little time remained for cleaning, laundry, and meal-planning. And my writing had to wait.

Although I tried to keep up with church activities, I spent less time reading my Bible during the week. In my busyness, I didn't have as much time for the Lord as before.

After several months, I began to wear down. My energy level dipped to a low I had never known, even in pregnancy. After arriving home very late from a party nearly every night, I had great difficulty getting my family off to work and school the next morning. Somehow we managed, but after they left I'd crawl back into bed for another hour or two of sleep.

Since Maryanne, who was only about three years old then, was still not in school, I would bring the portable television into the bedroom, close the door, and she would lay in bed with me and watch TV while I dozed away most of the morning.

This only happened once or twice a week at first. As time wore on, however, I wore down more and more. I started running a low-grade fever, and those mornings in bed became more frequent. Miraculously, our spunky little three-year-old became quite docile during that time. God's little gifts are merciful.

I knew the schedule was ruining my health, but I couldn't quit. The home party plan made it a self-perpetuating job, and I didn't want to turn my parties over to someone else. We needed the money.

I went to the doctor. He diagnosed fatigue (for that I paid thirty dollars?) and told me to rest. I tried. Sometimes my mother would come over and watch Maryanne, allowing me to sleep all day to get enough rest before another party that night.

One night I got lost attempting to come home a different route. Rain covered the windshield faster than the wipers could whisk it away, and I didn't see a familiar landmark until almost midnight. Then, taking another short-cut home, I stalled the car in the middle of a big, deep mud puddle. The motor refused to start again. Since we only had one car, my phone call to Steve required him to phone my brother-in-law to come and rescue me.

Scared, soaked, and exhausted, I wished I would never have to go out alone at night again. But with another party the next night, I knew the futility of my wish.

Repeated trips to the doctor brought no help until he ordered some rather sophisticated tests. The pathologist's report listed three possibilities:

A. hepatitis (which had already been ruled out by other tests);

B. some type of viral infection of the liver (similar to hepatitis);

C. early stages of alcohol or drug abuse.

My doctor laughed at the last alternative in the report. "That guy doesn't know you like I do," he quipped. "You don't touch nothin'! It must be a virus." (Famous last words.)

At least now I knew there was something *physically* wrong. I had begun to wonder if my illness was psychosomatic. But giving it a name didn't bring a cure. The doctor said I wasn't contagious and suggested no treatment other than rest.

I secretly hoped he would order me to stop working. But he knew our financial bind (didn't even charge us for some of the tests) and said I could work as much as I felt able. So I rested during the days and worked at night, all the time feeling worse, not better.

My spiritual strength drained as well. Sometimes I didn't even feel well enough to go to church. A strange coldness enveloped my spirit. I couldn't concentrate on my Bible readings—at times I didn't even want to. My prayers were self-centered. Prayers for relief and for some solution to my dilemma seemed to be just monologues. Occasionally the Lord sent encouragement through other Christians, but few knew of my struggle.

When I had service commitments to fulfill I would cry out to the Lord asking for His help in singing or whatever else I had to do. He graciously gave me a measure of peace and help, but soon I was back in bed again, thoroughly exhausted and not sure why the Lord had allowed all this.

The virus ran its course in six weeks. The fever went down. Energy returned. I struggled for another two or three months trying to decide whether or not to quit working. I felt better physically, the financial situation had improved somewhat, but my spiritual health still yo-yoed. The decision was not easy.

I began to realize, however, that this was not what *God* wanted for me. I hadn't consulted Him much about taking the job in the first place. It *seemed* right, so I did it. Disobedience—not following His plans for me or consulting Him about *my* plans—is the only explanation I have for the "coldness" I felt during that period.

Slowly, I began to look for *His* answer to my problem. Steve wouldn't tell me what to do. I had to decide. I enjoyed the parties. Our budget still needed help. Did the Lord have another way of meeting that need? Did He have other plans for me at that time? Searching diligently, I asked, "Lord, where are You in all this? What do You want me to do?" I really wanted to know.

In Jeremiah 29:13 the Lord makes a promise. "And you will seek Me and find Me, when you search for Me with all your heart" (NASB). I wish I could carve that promise on my brain so I will never forget it! While looking for Him, I did find Him, and He also provided the wisdom to make the decision. James 1:5 promises that if any of us lack wisdom we should ask God, "who gives generously to all without finding fault, and it will be given to him."

I didn't know how the Lord would resolve our financial problem, but I did know that He wanted me to spend more time in the writing ministry He had given me. And I knew He didn't want me misusing the body He had given me. I had to trust Him for what I *didn't* know.

A few months later the Lord opened a new opportunity for my writing which provided a small amount of financial help. The Lord proved Himself faithful to meet our needs when we looked to Him for the answer.

11 A Rainbow to Warm the Cold

Whether the coldness we feel is of our own doing or seems to come for no reason (which is more common than most Christians like to admit), God will make Himself known to us when we seek Him with all our heart.

I remember wondering many times why I couldn't be all fired up about the Lord all the time. I thought something was wrong with me. Maybe a contributing factor to my guilt was a statement I heard from the pulpit once: "If there ever was a time you felt closer to the Lord than you do now, you're in a backslidden condition," some preacher proclaimed.

There have been times I have felt so close to the Lord that I was sure He would call me home as He did Enoch. (See Genesis 5:24.) There are times when the Bible has so much meaning to me that I thrill at God's knowledge of my personal concerns. I get excited about Who He is and how blessed I am to belong to Him! I love Him intensely and would prefer to spend my whole day singing His praises.

But to be honest, there are days when, for no apparent reason, the Bible seems as dry as shredded wheat and just about as tasty. God's attributes seem totally irrelevant to my daily needs. I don't feel very loving toward Him. I just feel blah!

I don't think sin is always the cause. During

some of these dry periods I have agonized, sometimes for months, pleading with God for an answer. What is it, Lord? What have I done (or not done)? Why don't I *feel* right? Why can't I love You as I should? Why don't I feel totally enamored with Your Word? Why are my prayers so empty?

"I never asked you to base your relationship with Me on feelings," He seemed to say. "I called you to discipline, but you act as if Christianity is a religion of emotion. I called you to self-sacrifice; you're looking for self-gratification. I called you to faith; you're looking for feelings."

Sometimes I feel like a hypocrite when I read my Bible or sing a praise-filled choir anthem at church when my heart really doesn't *feel* like praising. But, rather than hypocrisy, I think this is the truest test of faith.

Many of our problems with emotional-level Christianity are caused by the way our society has come to define love—as a warm, mushy feeling that comes over us and renders us incapable of rational thinking. So when we talk about "Christian" love we confuse those who only understand society's definition of the term.

Is "warm and mushy" Christianity the kind that Jesus taught?

Evangelicals have emphasized for years that Christianity is not a religion, it is a relationship— a loving, personal relationship with the Lord Jesus Christ. And that it is! The basis of all our faith is love, but our love is based on *facts,* not warm, mushy feelings.

Yet we club ourselves over the head with guilt because we don't *feel* a certain way. We women, I think, are more susceptible to this than men are.

In his book *What Wives Wish Their Husbands Knew About Women*, Dr. James Dobson, noted psychologist and author, says this: "An effort has been underway for the past few years to prove that men and women are identical, except for the ability to bear children. Radical feminists have vigorously (and foolishly) asserted that the only distinction between the sexes is culturally and environmentally produced. Nothing could be farther from the truth; males and females differ biochemically, anatomically, and emotionally. In truth, they are unique in every cell of their bodies, for men carry a different chromosomal pattern than women."

God created women with a more sensitive emotional nature than men. And He had a purpose in doing so. As the gender of the species capable of child-bearing, we have a built-in emotional make-up that enables us to feel deeply, comfort sympathetically, and love devotedly. Some would resent being put in that kind of a box, but I praise the Lord for its security.

As I see it, the problems come when we base our actions entirely on feelings. There is no scriptural basis for that. In fact, Jesus said, "If anyone loves me, he [or she—here the gender doesn't matter] will *obey* my teaching. My Father will love him, and we will come to him and make our home with him" (John 14:23 italics mine).

That's another promise!

Our relationship to Christ doesn't change because our feelings change. He asks for obedience whether we feel like being obedient or not. I know how I react when my children (bless their little hearts) don't *feel* like doing what I tell them to do, and their feelings do not change my expectations of them.

Fortunately, God is holy and doesn't react as we do. I know it must grieve Him when we rationalize that there's no need to read our Bibles because we don't feel like it. It must really hurt Him when we neglect our prayer time because we don't sense His receptivity. How can He bear to hear us questioning our relationship with Him simply because we no longer feel the "glow"?

If you love me, do what I tell you to do, Jesus says, *regardless of how you feel. Then God the Father will show you what true love is. We'll come to you in a special way to make our presence known in your life* [paraphrase mine].

Not feelings—reality.

That's where discipline and faith come in. We need God's power of discipline in our lives to do what we know is right even if it doesn't "feel good." And we need the faith to believe that whether we see immediate results and blessings or not, we must obey.

The comforting and stabilizing factor is that *God* does not change. His feelings do not fluctuate from day to day as ours do. Jeremiah

31:3 says that He loves us with an everlasting love.

"Because God wanted to make the *unchanging* nature of his purpose very clear to the heirs of what was promised, he confirmed it with an oath. God did this so that . . . we who have fled to take hold of the hope offered to us may be greatly encouraged. We have this hope as an anchor for the soul, firm and secure" (Hebrews 6:17–19, italics mine).

I remember how the most popular little girl in our grade school used to manipulate the rest of us on the playground. "If you'll do this for me," she would say, "I'll be your friend." Or "If you don't play my way, I won't let you be my friend anymore." God isn't like that. He does not change. We can hang on to him and know He will not give up on us. No matter how fickle we may be, He is unchanging.

On the other hand, some of the emotional coldness we feel may be a diversionary tactic of the Enemy and his forces. Satan certainly doesn't want us to feel good and happy and secure in our relationship with the Lord. But as we keep seeking Him and obeying Him, regardless of our feelings, we can be assured that He is with us, working everything together for good. (See Romans 8:28.)

Indigo
Section

Moods

Now there was a castle, called Doubting Castle,
the owner whereof was Giant Despair . . .
> —*John Bunyan,* The Pilgrim's Progress

12 A Rainbow for a Sesame Street Mom

When my three children were preschoolers, there were days that my chief goal was *survival*. Yet for some reason the *real* stress didn't set in until the older two were in school. I had never been one to plunk the children down in front of "Sesame Street" or "Mister Rogers" for hours, but our third child became much better acquainted with Kermit, Big Bird, Grover, and Mr. Snuffalopagus than her siblings were.

Maybe I was numb when they were all home or maybe my memory has conveniently blocked out that era, but I don't remember things being so hectic then. When the other two went to school, though, Maryanne wanted my attention constantly.

We had some nice times together going for walks, reading stories, making cookies, collecting brightly colored leaves in the fall, and going shopping. (Actually, I haven't decided whether the shopping was a good or bad experience.)

As much as I would have liked to play games all day, however, other things needed to be done. So Maryanne began to create her own little play world. She learned to read early and found a wonderful new universe open to her there. Musical ability also began to awaken in her. That, coupled with her newly found reading skills, often led her to her private sanctuary (the smallest room in the house) with stacks of my music books. There she would sit and sing contentedly for hours if we didn't interrupt her.

Naturally, she asked scores of endless questions. While I washed the dishes: "Mommy, why is water clear?" When we walked by the creek: "Mommy, how do ducks float?" While I painted the house trim: "Mommy, why do they call it summer?" From her seat in the grocery cart (and quite aware of my constant battle of the bulge): "Mommy, is this 'diet' toilet paper?"

Some days her imagination broke the tension of her constant questions and demands. One afternoon when Maryanne was about three and I was feeling a little "mothered out," my own mom came to spend the day with us (a weekly occurrence at that time). While Mom and I talked, we worked on some needlepoint. Maryanne disappeared for a short time, then re-emerged with one of my belts in her hand. To Maryanne, who is a born performer, almost anything can be used as a microphone if it's held just right. The belt was a new prop, but it worked very nicely. She held the gold buckle as if it were the head of the microphone, and the rest of the belt trailed down like the mike cord.

"Mommy, have you seen my pet snake?" Maryanne asked into the pretend microphone, quickly moving it from her mouth to mine.

Since I had no knowledge of any pet snakes in our house, either real or imaginary, I tried to hold back a snicker and replied, "No, Maryanne, I have not seen your pet snake."

She immediately whirled around to address (I

suppose) her imaginary audience. With face
aglow she proclaimed, "Did you hear that, folks?
Mommy—has not seen—*my pet snake!*"

I could hardly keep from laughing, but it only
got funnier, because she then took the "mike"
over to my mother, shoved it in front of *her* face,
and asked, "Gramma, have you seen my pet
snake?"

My mother was in stitches by now, but finally
managed to answer. "No, Maryanne. I haven't
seen your pet snake, either."

Again Maryanne whirled. "Did you hear that,
folks? Gramma—has not seen—*my pet snake,
either.*" She grinned so big I thought her teeth
were going to pop out.

I don't know what mean streak possessed me
at that moment, but I called my little performer
over to me and with the gravest sincerity said,
"Maryanne, I don't know how to tell you this,
but I think your pet snake is dead."

Immediately, her smile drooped to a pout. Her
lower lip began to tremble. I thought she was
going to cry. In slow motion she brought the belt
buckle up to that sad little mouth and in the most
mournful tone said, "Did you hear that, folks?"
(sniff, sniff) "Mommy thinks my pet snake—(she
could hardly bring herself to say it)—is—dead."

I couldn't stand it. I didn't want her to have a
breakdown. Unable to watch that sad little face
any longer, I motioned for her to bring the
"mike" to me again.

"I'm sorry, Maryanne," I said to the belt

buckle. "I think I was mistaken. I think your pet snake was just sleeping."

Instantly she whirled and was beaming again. "Did you hear that, folks?" she said excitedly. "Mommy says my pet snake is not dead. It was just sleeping!"

My mother and I laughed until tears came to our eyes. We had no idea where any of this little comedy sketch came from. It wasn't until a few months ago that I caught a short segment of "Sesame Street" in which Kermit the Frog was giving a news flash about various nursery rhymes. Acting as a reporter (with microphone), he interviewed Jack and Jill to determine how their terrible tumbling accident occurred. There in the middle of the sketch was Kermit saying, "Did you hear that, folks? . . ."

How easy it is to get so bogged down with the "naughtinesses" of our preschoolers that we can't enjoy their fun. Often my little ones were simply having fun or being silly when their behavior began to irritate me. Instead of joining with them, however, I pushed them aside or scolded them for the noise. I think the key to surviving those preschool years is to enter into the fun and laugh with them as much as possible.

"Children are a gift of the Lord," says Psalm 127:3 (NASB).

Some days they may not seem like a gift, or they may not seem to be a very *good* gift, but we have the Lord's word on it. Children *are* a gift of the Lord.

The funny times can relax a tired mom and

renew her strength for tough battles with pre-schoolers bent on naughtiness. And is there anything that brings out more naughtiness in a preschooler than a grocery cart?

When one of our children was quite small, she learned the most effective weapon in the battle of the wills. A simple swat on the behind for disobedience evoked the loudest, sharpest, most piercing cry ever heard. And she knew her behavior was most effective in the grocery store. "Honey, leave the jar of jelly in the cart. Don't play with it; it might—"

Crash!

A slapped hand. A long penetrating wail. And suddenly a whole storeful of people is staring at me, ready to have me arrested for child abuse or disturbing the peace.

The child enjoyed the power. Many times I would give up instead of getting tougher. Some-times I would literally hand the child over to Steve and say, "You do something. I can't control this kid!" I soon learned that giving up was the worst thing I could have done. It not only encouraged the bad behavior and crying, it also sabotaged my authority.

The crying tactic was also effective in church or around my friends—actually, any place Mom could be royally embarrassed.

One day I was sitting on the lawn outside the auditorium of a Bible conference where my "crying machine" had been a disturbance. A woman (who had successfully raised six children) sympathized. "I used to worry about those tears after spankings too," she said. "But then I found this verse: 'Chasten thy son while there is hope, and let not thy soul spare for his crying'" (Proverbs 19:18 KJV).

As I listened to this woman, I took the verse to mean "despair not for the crying." It helped me that day to do what I knew was right—to discipline whether the crying got to me or not. But the woman also cautioned me that discipline must come in love.

When I read the verse later in other translations I found that my presumed meaning was not actually there (although it may be implied). The New International Version puts it this way: "Discipline your son, for in that there is hope; do not be a willing party to his death." The Moffatt translation says, "Chastise your son . . . and do not let him run to ruin."

In a day when child abuse is rampant and authorities suspect thousands of cases go unreported every year, we certainly need to be careful that we don't get carried away by our emotions when we discipline our children. But neither should we be intimidated by our little ones. When they need a reminder that their behavior is inappropriate, God has provided a built-in "cushiony" spot for that reminder.

Dr. James Dobson advocates differentiating between childish irresponsibility and deliberate disobedience—spilling milk at the dinner table (again) versus puddle jumping in new shoes (after you had told the child to stay inside). Dr. Dobson suggests that a spanking (in the appropriate place) only be administered for deliberate disobedience. We have tried to follow that guideline, but with preschoolers it's sometimes difficult to differentiate between the two behaviors.

One of our preschoolers once "dusted" our bedspread with half a large container of baby powder. The bedspread wasn't washable, so I finally vacuumed it! For weeks, every time I vacuumed, the whole house smelled like the nursery.

Before we spank, we try to make sure our child understands what he or she did wrong and why they are receiving a spanking. Afterward, we reassure them of our love with a hug and a little loving conversation.

The main point, as I see it from Scripture, is that the parents take charge and, as Moffatt translated it, "not let them run to ruin."

A very special rainbow promise I cling to here is Proverbs 22:6: "Train up a child in the way he should go, even when he is old he will not depart from it" (NASB).

We are responsible for the training. *God* is responsible for the results.

Our children's spiritual training is our highest priority. We cannot leave it to a Sunday school teacher or Christian school curriculum.

Do our children know God? Are they learning to love Him as we do? Even during their preschool days, they're not too young to learn God's principles and His love. Some preschoolers have enough understanding to put their trust in Christ as their Savior.

We need to be careful, however, that we don't expect more maturity from them than we do from ourselves. It's easy to expect them to be more mature than their years allow.

I remember a shopping trip when one of our little ones (much to my surprise) hadn't needed a reprimand once.

"Mommy," she said, "I've been good today, haven't I?"

"Yes, Punky, you have *really* been good today. You've stayed right with me. You didn't get into anything. You've really been terrific." Then I went too far. "Now, why can't you behave nicely like that *all* the time?"

She looked at me incredulously. "All the time?" she asked. "You mean all the days and all the nights?"

"Uh-huh."

"Now that's what I call hard work!" she replied.

Although we need to beware of our expectations, we also need to bring the spiritual dimension into every area of our family life.

The first time I met our son's kindergarten teacher she was bursting to tell me all about Greg. She had been his "two-by-two" buddy on their zoo field trip. As they walked around the zoo grounds on a lovely fall day, five-year-old Greg clutched his teacher's hand a little tighter, looked up into the sky and said, "Isn't this a beautiful day our God has made?"

Deuteronomy 11:18–20 tells us that we are to lay up God's words in our hearts and minds—to memorize them. "Teach them to your children," it says, "talking about them when you sit at home [that's when *you* sit—preschoolers don't know how], and when you walk along the road [drive around town on errands?], when you lie down and when you get up [naptime? I needed one too!]."

If we weave scriptural teachings and promises into our family routines, God promises us a special blessing (v. 21).

Evidently our little Greg had learned something. In his own precocious way he, in turn, talked about it with his teacher as *he* "walked along the path."

God's promises are trustworthy in life-and-death situations, but they are just as dependable for squabbles and daily routine. We can teach our children the promises and show them how to grasp those rainbows and hang on. God is as faithful to our children as He is to us. That we can count on!

No matter how tough the trial of our patience or how often we feel we're not getting through, He says, *Hang in there. You can survive—and even have fun doing it. I am with you and I'll bring growth and the best of all possible endings out of it all.*

"Behold, children *are* a gift of the Lord."

13 A Rainbow for Depression

Maybe the reason I don't remember much about "the days of three preschoolers" is because I was living in my own personal Great Depression. I felt as if I had fallen into a deep well and was trapped underneath the bucket at the bottom. That well of depression became an all too familiar place.

Health problems early in our marriage and having to quit work (causing bills that I couldn't help to pay) all added up. Better times came, but then so did another bout with ill health or some newly discovered inadequacy that would plop me back into the well again.

Then the children came—one by one, adding responsibilities I hadn't known before. Wanting to be "the perfect mother," I was constantly afraid that I would make a big mistake and someone would catch me.

Our church situation was stressful during that time too. We were one of only a handful of couples trying to maintain a small, inner-city church with a Sunday school of up to one hundred kids. There was no full-time pastor. Two services on Sunday mornings and one in the evening required our attendance. Although I only play the piano by ear (and not very well at that), I played for the services because there wasn't anyone else to do it. I also accompanied the youth choir.

Both my husband and I taught Sunday school

classes, and he was superintendent for a while. We both worked with the "Kids' Club" one night a week and attended Bible study on Wednesday nights. Steve also went to a men's prayer meeting every Saturday at 7:30 A.M., and I shared teaching responsibilities for a ladies' Bible study every week, served as church missionary correspondent, and worked as president of an inter-church ladies' missionary sewing group.

It seemed as though we were never home. We wanted time with our family. We needed time alone. We were constantly tired. In addition, I was struggling with depression over personality conflicts within the church and the demands put upon us. And my attitude only complicated the problem.

Once or twice someone in the church handed us some money so we could get away for a weekend, for which I was very grateful. I don't know what I would have done without it. But soon our very normal children were once again causing the usual amount of stress, I got behind in my work again, and more conflicts went unresolved. Some days I did little but cry. So much pressure! So little time to myself. I seldom had the car during the day and rarely got out of the house other than for church responsibilities.

I began making excuses to stay home. (Funny how quickly another pianist emerged.) The more I stayed home, the less I wanted to be around other people. People ask questions and expect a person to smile all the time. I didn't feel like smiling. I'd often been told I wore my heart on my sleeve, so I feared going out and letting people see how battered it really was. I was supposed to be a leader, and leaders weren't supposed to have problems.

I stayed home more and more.

My writing career was beginning to bud, and I had assignments and deadlines that were hard to juggle around the needs of my youngsters. Housework seemed pointless, yet it constantly loomed over me. But why should I work so hard when it would all get messy again in less than twenty-four hours? There were days when the simple act of making my bed was a major accomplishment.

To make matters worse, I was struggling with a weight problem. During my pregnancies I gained very little weight, but shortly after each delivery I gained twenty pounds, then added an additional twenty in the years that followed. Physical activities and exercise were "too much work," so I avoided them as much as possible.

In our inner-city church, the young people with whom we worked dressed in jeans and sweatshirts or casual tops. So I felt no need or desire to dress up. Shopping for clothes was depressing anyway. Very few stores carry size "huge."

My self-esteem, which was rather fragile to begin with, soon shattered. I felt like a failure whenever my children disobeyed or the meatloaf was a little black around the edges or someone dropped by and found the house a mess.

One evening I was so confused, hurt, and full

of self-pity that I took the car (leaving my husband and children wondering what had gotten into me) and, with tears in my eyes, drove aimlessly through the city. At last I came to a parkway by the river where I could be alone, try to get my head together, and regain control of my emotions.

Depression (in various forms) has been a well I've fallen into many times over the years. Its causes have ranged from pressure to fatigue to "the blues" (with accompanying witch-like behavior) that many women experience during their monthly cycle. It can be a let-down after an exciting or emotional experience or simply a feeling of inadequacy, insecurity, or inferiority. Depression has crept up on me, in its milder forms, like a house cat on a hunt. In more severe cases, it has pounced on me like a panther. But either way, it always causes my emotions to fluctuate between anger and "poor me." The simple question "Mom, what are we having for supper?" could send me into tears or a tirade.

One night as I lay on my bed, crying over my inability to cope, I remembered something strange. A few weeks earlier, on a trip to visit my in-laws in Wisconsin, a green-and-white highway sign caught my attention. "Victory—Unincorporated," it read.

The sign was a highway marker for the tiny, unincorporated town of Victory, Wisconsin. Most people probably drive through the town without even noticing it. A few houses dot the hillside across Highway 35 from the Mississippi River, and peeling paint marks a combination post office/gas station. But the highway sign left an impression on me.

For some reason, on that night of tearful depression when I had reached a breaking point, the green-and-white sign flashed through my mind: "Victory—Unincorporated."

Yes, it meant the town was too small to organize into a corporation. But as I thought about it, a double meaning emerged. Victory over mountainous problems was freely available. I simply had to incorporate it—to make it an integral part of my daily life.

Certain verses came to mind. "This is the victory that has overcome the world, even our faith" (1 John 5:4). "Now faith is being sure of what we hope for and certain of what we do not see" (Hebrews 11:1).

The word *victory* reminded me of an Easter Sunday sermon in which our pastor had emphasized the power of the resurrection: "I *can*—in the power of the resurrection." When the all-powerful Christ triumphed over death, His resurrection was the ultimate victory. In Christ's omnipotence He triumphed over death and every other temptation and problem facing us. He lives within us—within *me!*

"Give up! Reach up! Through faith accept the victory I've promised and incorporate it into your own life," the Lord seemed to be saying.

That one road sign prompted a "U-turn" in my outlook.

The depressing circumstances did not vanish

instantly, but I had a tool for handling them. God showed me some practical ways to avoid falling into the well of depression so often.

First of all, I needed to meet with my siblings in Christ whether I felt like it or not. This meant forcing myself to get out of bed some Sundays, but I knew I had to obey the Lord's command: "Let us not give up meeting together, as some are in the habit of doing, but let us encourage one another" (Hebrews 10:25). I had to shift my attitude from "Poor me" to "How can I help *you?*"

All those personality conflicts did not melt away, but God gave us the grace to work things through where we could and to accept the differences that wouldn't dissolve.

I also had to learn that I was responsible to God first and that He never asked me to be a slave to the expectations of others.

Another project the Lord (and my doctor) gave me was to lose some of the extra weight that was contributing to my sluggishness. It has been extremely difficult, and I've done a lot of yo-yoing on the bathroom scale, but as I write this I'm more than forty pounds lighter than I was. Again, it has been a matter of making myself "do it" whether I felt like it or not. I've asked the Lord for His help, but I can't expect Him to do it for me. He helps me as I'm willing to make it happen.

Sometimes I blow it, and I still have a long way to go, but I'm well on my way. I *can* get down to a healthy weight in the power of the resurrection (and with a little patience).

One of the requirements of my weight-loss program was exercise. I started with walking, then jogging. But I kept feeling as though my organs were all going to get mixed up and wouldn't be able to find their right places again. Back to walking. Finally the Lord opened a way for me to swim three or four times a week as well.

Exercising on a regular basis helped my outlook. I felt better, looked better (because I wanted my clothing to complement my progress), and was able to think more clearly. My self-esteem was taking shape again, and I was becoming a better wife and mother.

Although there were some very definite spiritual causes for my depression, there were also physical causes.

I think Paul's training advice to Timothy is a type of promise from God too. He says, "Physical training *is* of some value . . ." (1 Timothy 4:8 AMPLIFIED). Exercise is not an end in itself, but it does play an important role in having a healthy body, mind, and spirit. When I'm feeling depressed, many times I can (if I take the time to think about it) easily pinpoint the cause: I haven't had any fresh air or exercise for a few days (weeks?).

My husband has been amazed at the difference it makes. A couple of months ago I was shut up in the house for several weeks with one child after another suffering various winter maladies.

On a Saturday afternoon I lay down, feeling a little ill myself but not really understanding the cause. Steve came upstairs and asked if I wanted to go for a walk.

"A walk?" I asked. "The snow is three feet deep, and it's nearly zero out there!"

"Sharie is working on a project for school, and she needs to go for a walk in a wooded area and make a chart about living things," he said. "Why don't we all go together? You'd probably feel better if you got outside for a while."

I knew he was right. After only a few minutes of tromping through the snow and sinking down to my thighs, laughing so hard I could hardly get up again, dodging snowballs from my son, and trying to find other "living things" that were crazy enough to be out there in the cold, I did feel a lot better.

I'll never be a marathon runner or make the Olympic swimming team, but I know now how important a little exercise is.

Even more important, though, is the remainder of the promise in 1 Timothy 4:8. Paul says that "godliness [spiritual training] is useful and of value in everything and in every way, for it holds promise for the present life and also for the life which is to come" (AMPLIFIED).

God promises us that godliness is even more transforming than physical exercise. It is useful and of value in *everything*, and in *every* way. Godliness transforms our daily routine and affirms our life in heaven someday. This made me realize how much I had been neglecting my spiritual exercises of reading and applying God's Word daily and of conversing with Him in prayer. It had been a vicious cycle. I got busy, neglected my spiritual disciplines, dropped into that well of depression (which made me "not feel like" spending time with the Lord, which ruined my appetite for spiritual food), and on and on it went. I sank lower and lower into the well, certain that I would drown any moment.

I learned that godliness is simply God-like-ness. I needed to *know* more about Him if I was going to *be* like Him. The Bible was my best resource (whether I felt like reading it or not).

I recommitted myself to keeping a notebook of what I was learning as I spent time with the Lord each day. I recorded some of my prayer thoughts and some of the insights the Lord gave me as I read His Word. I also noted my frustrations and areas of need. Starting in Matthew, a gospel account I hadn't studied much before, I tried to learn as much as I could about the character of the Lord Jesus Christ. As God's Son (and truly God Himself), Jesus was the perfect model of godliness. I wanted to get to know Him better— to find out how he reacted in daily situations. I wanted to follow His example—to be like Him.

I often followed my quiet time with my daily walk, using that half-hour of walking time as an opportunity to pray for people or situations I may not otherwise have taken time to pray for.

Memorizing verses of Scripture on the attrib-utes or characteristics of God—love, holiness,

grace, faithfulness, omnipotence, omniscience—
was another meaningful exercise.

Gradually I realized how important God was to
me. I found out that as a child of God some of
His characteristics were available for *my* life. His
power, wisdom, love, and holiness were mine if I
would yield to Him my "rights" to do things my
own way. I could know His grace and faithfulness if I would look for it instead of complain-
ing and feeling sorry for myself when things
didn't work out as I thought they should. It was
like breathing fresh air on a snowy romp through
the woods! Although I still wrestle with carving
out that half hour or more every day for a quiet
time with the Lord, I know I need it. I have a
different perspective on the problems of the day
if I've spent that time with Him.

My bouts with depression come less often
now, and they don't last as long as they once
did. Depression is a symptom, not a disease. And
since its causes are so varied, I have to understand what's causing it before I can have relief.
I've also been learning that I don't have to stay in
that well of depression. With Christ's help I can
ride the bucket to the top and climb out!

14 A Rainbow for the Overscheduled

It was bound to happen. I should have known. Some people struggle to find the reason for their existence. I don't. There are days when I feel quite certain that my sole purpose in life is to prove Murphy's law: If anything can go wrong, it will.

When my husband became Chief Ranger for the Boys' Brigade program in our church, I offered to be the hostess for any meetings he might want to have with the other Rangers. Last year he had the meetings at church because we were in the process of moving. This fall he invited the men to our home for the organizational meeting.

All would have been fine except that other deadlines and my expertise in the field of procrastination caused me to leave the house-cleaning and dessert preparations for the day of the meeting.

That's why I say it was bound to happen. When I awoke that morning I felt a little sluggish. By mid-morning, after getting all three kids off to school and starting the dessert for that night, I felt terrible.

"Lord, I can't afford a day in bed today. There are fifteen men descending on my living room tonight and this place is a mess!"

I crawled upstairs to assess the bathroom's cleaning needs. Then I noticed the open *Daily*

Light—a book of daily Scripture readings arranged by subject. I sometimes use it as a supplement to my regular quiet time, but I don't read it every day.

I flipped to the page for that date.

"Well, what do You have to say for a day like today, Lord?" I asked out loud.

Glancing at the top of the page I read, "He maketh me to lie down in green pastures" (Psalm 23:2 KJV).

Oh, good, I thought, *I can crawl back in bed and forget about it all.* (I have a green flowery bedspread. That's close to green pastures, isn't it?) Maybe if I went back to bed for a while I would feel better later and could do just a little "get–by" cleaning.

Then I realized that I had been reading the page for the *evening* of that day. The morning's Scripture began with a wonderful promise. "Wait on the Lord: be of good courage, and he shall strengthen thine heart" (Psalm 27:14 KJV).

I started to giggle but read on. "He giveth power to the faint; and to them that have no might he increaseth strength" (Isaiah 40:29 KJV).

"I am with thee . . . I will strengthen thee; yea, I will help thee; yea, I will uphold thee with the right hand of my righteousness" (Isaiah 41:10 KJV).

But when I got to the last verse I laughed right out loud. "For ye have need of patience, that, after ye have done the will of God, ye might receive the promise" (Hebrews 10:36 KJV).

What promise? "He maketh me to lie down . . ." of course.

"Oh, Lord, what a beautiful sense of humor You have," I said. "I can lie down after You've given me the strength to do my task: to make our home look its best for my husband's guests. Okay, where's the rag box?"

My symptoms didn't magically disappear, but I knew the Lord understood. He helped me think of ways to do most of my work sitting down. When I did have to be up straightening and putting things away, I did them in short segments of time. I took sit-down breaks with my feet propped up while I sorted through papers and mail. Then I made piles on the floor, consolidating my trips to put things away.

When the children came home from school I let them know I wasn't feeling well and enlisted their help for the cleaning and straightening chores they knew how to do. Amazement upon amazement, they didn't even complain. I finished making the dessert while I heated some chili I had made the day before.

The meeting went well. The men loved my dessert. The children felt needed. And when the Lord of humor made me lie down in my green pasture later that night I didn't have any trouble falling asleep.

The underlying reason for that whole episode is my predisposition to overschedule my life. Being a compulsive "yes" person naturally leads to overscheduling. A close cousin to Superwoman, overscheduling robs us of both energy and peace of mind.

Three major deadlines in one month? Sure. I'll make it.

Entertain missionaries for dinner the day after we get home from vacation? Why not?

A field trip with twenty kindergarteners in the afternoon and a speaking engagement in the evening? Of course. How can I say no?

How *can* I say no?

Sometimes I think it just takes practice. Maybe I should take lessons. Put your tongue on the roof of your mouth, Joyce. Form the "n," then follow through with a big round "o." Perhaps it's pride that keeps me from saying such a simple little word.

But it's not, of course, one simple little word. I have to be diplomatic. To simply say no would be rude. I must have a good excuse for not driving the football team to their out-of-town game next Saturday. To tell them that I already have several commitments that weekend would sound like a phony excuse. Everybody's busy. They *need* me. And so I rush from one appointment to another, from one area of service to another, from one activity to another, joining the hectic rat race common to us all.

But there is another reason I get over-scheduled: I *enjoy* doing many things. And since the Lord has gifted me in a number of these areas, am I not responsible to Him to use all my gifts?

My dad used to tell a joke that humorously

points out the futility of overburdening ourselves with numerous activities and responsibilities:

A woman fixing her husband a midnight snack asked him, "Honey, do you want me to cut this pizza into six pieces or eight?"

"Better cut it into six," the husband replied. "I don't think I could eat eight."

It's a groaner, but it makes a point.

Somehow we have been convinced that this strange logic is true. But it's not. There are no extra brownie points in heaven for cutting ourselves into smaller pieces. Scripture does say, however, that "Unto whomsoever much is given, of him shall be much required: and to whom men have committed much, of him they will ask the more" (Luke 12:48 KJV).

And people do keep asking more and more and more. Before we know it we are over-scheduled, hassled, and don't really savor life as God intended.

At some point we must say, "This is what I will do. I can only be cut up into this many pieces— no more. I'm very sorry, but I won't be able to do that for you." We might then suggest some-one else who could handle the task. No *one* person can do everything, and there are others who may be equally talented or perhaps even better-equipped to do that task. They may be a bit shy or need a little coaxing, but they're there.

God's little rainbow for me in this has been Psalm 37:4: "Delight yourself in the Lord and he will give you the desires of your heart."

That's a conditional promise. *If* we delight

ourselves in the Lord or look to Him for our
fulfillment, satisfaction, and joy, then He will give
us the desires of our heart. To me that means He
will give me the *right* desires for my heart. Forget
the side-trips and the interests that only lead to
overscheduling and are not in the Lord's plan.
His plan for each of us is different.

The next verses complete the thought. "Commit your way to the Lord; trust in him and he will
do this: He will make your righteousness shine
like the dawn . . ." (Psalm 37:5–6). That is
fantastic!

It sounds so peaceful—so unhurried—so like
Him! But it takes commitment. Not *over*-
commitment, but commitment to what we determine before Him that He wants us to do. Then if
we trust Him to take care of our pride and our
fear of what others will think and even our side
interests, He'll do it. And our righteousness will
shine as a testimony to others that we *don't have
to be hassled, harried housewives.* We can be at
peace!

Violet
Section

Royalty

Rosamond then understood
that the mere calling herself a princess,
without having anything to show for it,
was of no use.

—*George MacDonald,* The Lost Princess

15 A Rainbow for a Princess

The story of Cinderella and the Prince is one of my favorite fairy tales. What a wretched life that poor girl lived. No one cared for her. She lacked self-esteem, and she was unquestionably over-worked (no way out of *that* kind of overscheduling problem). If anyone had a reason to be depressed, Cinderella did. Then along came Prince Charming. By marrying Cinderella, he liberated her from a dreary existence and changed her from a commoner to a princess!

That's a good analogy of what happened to me when I found the Prince of Peace (the Lord Jesus Christ) and took Him for my own. I didn't live in ragged clothes like Cinderella, but my spiritual condition was ragged. The Bible says that without Christ in our lives "all our righteous acts are like filthy rags" (Isaiah 64:6). I tried hard to be holy and good, but I couldn't do it on my own. Yet unlike Cinderella, who had to be made beautiful (by magic) *before* she met the Prince, I came to God as I was—sinful, self-willed, and totally unable to meet His standards. God loved me anyway. He made the transformation in my life, and He didn't even need a magic wand.

I was a commoner before I trusted Christ, but I believed the Bible's promise that "to all who received him, to those who believed in his name, he gave the right to become children of God" (John 1:12). The Bible also speaks of those who have trusted Christ as making up His "bride." Since God is King, and His Son, Jesus Christ, is the Prince of Peace, as part of His bride I am a princess in *the* Royal Family.

Cinderella left her life of rags and moved to the palace of the Prince. When we become Christians, we aren't immediately transported to our new home, but we have God's promise that we *will* be there someday to live with Him forever.

The apostle John said, "I write these things to you who believe in the name of the Son of God so that you may *know* that you have eternal life" (1 John 5:13). We don't have to guess about our salvation or wonder if we've done enough to merit a heavenly home. God promises that if we have believed on the Lord Jesus Christ as the one who can save us, we can count on an eternity with Him. That is exciting!

I didn't understand this princess idea immediately, though. I knew I was a Christian, and I knew I would be with the Lord Jesus when I died, but it took me a while to appreciate the realm in which I could be living.

When I began to realize the potential of being the Prince's princess, my behavior began to change. No overnight realization nor one specific instance brought me to this new way of thinking. Instead I began a gradual process of finding out who God was making me to be. I began to discover that there was no reason to live "under the circumstances." I could live above them. Circumstances didn't have to control my life.

I gained a sense of destiny—of purpose. I had

a royal heritage, and the King's business was my business as well. It was my responsibility and privilege to bring others to meet the Prince and to show them how to enter His kingdom.

I also found out, however, that royalty is always in the public eye. I had no spiritual "diplomatic immunity" to trouble or sin, and people watch constantly. Sometimes out of curiosity. Sometimes to try to trip us.

When Prince Charles announced his engagement to Lady Diana Spencer, the whole world began to watch the two closely. Reporters hounded Lady Diana day and night, waiting outside her Kensington flat or the kindergarten where she worked, eager to get a candid shot for their publications. Lady Diana was soon dubbed "Shy Di" because of her attempts to avoid the press.

Sometimes in the middle of a trying situation I feel the pressure to react "just right." *If I don't handle this properly,* I think, *people won't be interested in the faith I say I have.*

Other times I worry that I'm not setting a good example for our children. One Monday while our kids were out of school for spring vacation I foolishly tried to get a little writing done. My office is part of the unfinished laundry room in the basement, just on the other side of the furnace from the washing machine and dryer.

As I wrote, my youngest daughter leaned against the desk, watched me for a while, then asked, "Mommy, what's that noise?"

Having tuned out most distractions, I replied, "What noise?"

"This noise," she said, pointing to the water softener only two feet from my desk.

I looked up and saw a tiny thread of water trickling down the side of the water softener. A small puddle had already accumulated on the floor, and in the puddle sat a box of thirty or forty sample magazines (a freelance writer's necessity). I knew I had to stop the leak, but my knowledge of anything mechanical is virtually nil.

I called Steve at work and jokingly asked him if he remembered what we now refer to as "Black Monday," a day a few years ago when our water heater burst, the basement flooded, and the car broke down (not once, but twice) all on the same day.

I shouldn't have joked about it.

Steve suggested I get a screwdriver and tighten the large blue plastic screw (from which the water softener seemed to be leaking). I did exactly what he told me, tightening it only a little bit. Now, instead of a trickle, a fine spray came out. "Turn it back the other way—just a little," he instructed.

I turned it back a tiny bit. The screw popped out. Water sprayed into my face, all over my desk, and out the door onto the carpeting in the family room. "Oh, no! Oh, no!" I started yelling. "It's spraying all over the place!"

"Turn the main water valve off," Steve shouted.

"Where is it?" I dropped the phone and

hunted all over the laundry room, trying to find the wheel that would shut off this inside water hydrant.

By now my hair, clothes, and skin were drenched. My shoes squished as I walked through the water. I panicked. I couldn't find any water valve!

Everything on my desk was dripping—Bibles, reference books, manuscripts, file folders, unanswered correspondence. I was sure everything was ruined. I sloshed around and around the laundry room, frantically turning one valve after another. But none of them did any good. "I can't find it. I can't find it!" I cried over and over. "Oh, Lord, please help me." Crying seemed the only thing to do.

My daughter picked up the phone. "Daddy says to tell you he's coming home," she relayed.

"A lot of good that'll do," I cried. "It'll take him more than half an hour. We'll all be drowned by then!"

Our son went to find a neighbor who might know where the water valve was. The water kept rising.

I finally had the presence of mind to move the things on my desk out of the constant barrage of water. Every time I went into my office to take another load, it was like someone had turned a garden hose on me, right in the face. My stomach felt sick each time I saw something else that was soaked. Wet storage boxes, stacked three or four high, needed to be moved. My face was as wet with tears as it was with soft water.

After a few minutes my neighbor came and found the shut-off valve. The water stopped. Although I was extremely grateful, I felt so sick about everything that was ruined that I couldn't stop crying.

My neighbor helped the kids get some towels to start sopping up the water that had saturated the family room carpeting around the doorway. "Is there anything else I can do?" she asked.

I was still crying. All I could think about was the mess. "I don't even know," I sniffed.

"Lord, please help me," I prayed again. "I'm not dealing with this very well."

After my neighbor left I began the clean-up. I couldn't believe what had happened. If that other day of disasters was Black Monday, what could we call this Monday?

I wasn't physically or emotionally ready for something like this. We had had a long, tiring weekend that had ended with my participation in an exciting but exhausting performance of Handel's *Messiah* the night before. I got to bed quite late.

I asked my kids to pray for me. I wasn't coping well at all. As I strung a clothesline around the laundry room, using clothespins to hang up envelopes and papers to dry, I felt more like the ragged, overworked Cinderella than any kind of a princess.

I should sing, I told myself. *It will make me feel better and be a good example for the kids.* But I couldn't sing. Some of the music from *The Messiah,* however, kept running through my mind: "Who is the King of Glory? Who is the King of Glory? The Lord strong and mighty!" I drew strength from that beautiful, triumphant song, and God reminded me of His promise that He was with me, even then.

I didn't handle the whole disaster as well as I should have, but I honestly don't know what I would have done if I hadn't had His help. God knows we are human. He knows how frail we are. In Psalm 103:14 David says that "He [the Lord] knows how we are formed, he remembers that we are dust." Our failures keep us humble and remind us we still need Him. If we blow it, He can even work *that* out for good in His own time.

A princess needs a sense of destiny that will enable her to see the larger picture. It is very important for me to remember that I can't live my life as I please. I belong to the King. His plans must dictate my actions.

Prince Charles captured the royal sense of destiny when he said, "I'm not a normal person, in the sense that I was born to be king. I've received a special education and training. I could never be a normal person because I've been prepared to reign over my subjects."

And Prince Charles' attitude falls right in line with the advice England's King George III gave his son: "The behaviour of royalty should be the exemplar for the nation."

The Bible says Christians are to be peculiar people (Titus 2:14 KJV). Some have taken that as license to call attention to themselves by acting weird or strange. But the use of the word *peculiar* in this case means "belonging particularly or exclusively to one." We use it to speak of animals or vegetation that is characteristic of an area. Some animals, like pumas, are peculiar to mountainous regions. Polar bears are peculiar to cold climates. Christians are peculiar to Christ. We belong exclusively to Him. We mirror His characteristics and live in *His* realm. It's that "godliness" quality again.

The New International Version translates Titus 2:13–14 this way: "Our great God and Savior, Jesus Christ . . . gave himself for us to redeem us from all wickedness and to purify for himself a people that are *his very own,* eager to do what is good" [italics mine].

But we can't consistently do what is good by ourselves.

Lady Diana was overwhelmed by all the fuss made over her and by the prospect of entering such a different life than she had been used to. She learned to handle it, saying, "With Prince Charles beside me, I cannot go wrong."

When doing what is right becomes difficult, and when circumstances overwhelm me, I'm learning that with Christ within me I cannot go wrong. God promises us that we are His "chosen people, a *royal* priesthood, a holy nation, a people belonging to God." He wants us to "declare the praises of him who called you out of darkness into his wonderful light" (1 Peter 2:9).

We are not ordinary people. We have a different life purpose. We are to bring honor and glory to the One Who saved us from our sin. Then He promises that we will reign with Him someday (Revelation 5:10). What a tremendous privilege, to rule along with the Creator of the universe—the almighty God! We can joyfully look forward to our eternity with Him.

A princess can hold her head high and revel in her heritage, but she must also be a woman of integrity. The trustworthiness of *God's* promises should make *us,* His children, people of integrity. When I make a promise to my children or a friend, I need to follow through. I have to be very careful what I promise. A child never forgets.

As representatives of the King, our word must be absolutely trustworthy. That's why I believe so strongly in the marriage commitment. When I made that vow on our wedding day, it was a promise. To break that promise is an affront to the God Who has never broken even one of His promises.

As a princess, no matter what may happen to me, whether personal loss or disappointment or trial or pain, I know that I belong to God and that He is in control. I know my real purpose. My destiny is assured.

The apostle John got excited about our position in Christ and declared, "How great is the love the Father has lavished on us, that we should be called children of God! And that is what we are!" Then John follows with a promise from God about our future. "Now we are children of God, and what we will be has not yet been made known. But we know that when he appears, we *shall* be like him, for we shall see him as he is" (1 John 3:1–2, italics mine). I can't wait!

16 Making the Rainbows Yours

These rainbows I've been discovering are great promises from an all-powerful, loving God, who cares about broken shoestrings as well as life-threatening situations. His promises are life-brightening rainbows that I have access to because I've trusted in the Lord Jesus Christ personally as my Savior.

God's wonderful rainbow promises are available to everyone who says, "I'm ready now to quit running my own life, Lord. I know that you agonized and died on that horrible cross to take the punishment for *my* sin. Thank You for dying for *me*. I accept You into my life. I want to live for You."

God has provided only one way to be right with Him. We may claim the promise of heaven or any of the other promises of Scripture only if we have accepted His forgiveness for ourselves. When we give Him control of our lives, we become His children and can trust Him to keep His word, no matter what. With God, a promise is a promise!

I have found Him to be absolutely trustworthy. We can depend on Him! "Praise be to the LORD. . . . Not one word has failed of all the good promises he gave" (1 Kings 8:56).

All through Scripture we have this confirmation: God keeps His promises!

Abraham trusted God. Romans 4:20–21 tells

us that "he [Abraham] did not waver through unbelief regarding the promise of God, but was strengthened in his faith and gave glory to God, being fully persuaded that God had power to do what he had promised." The King James Version says, "being fully persuaded that, what he [God] had promised, he was able also to perform."

"And so, after he [Abraham] had patiently endured, he obtained the promise" (Hebrews 6:15 KJV).

Abraham's wife, Sarah, also discovered that God could be trusted. "Sarah herself . . . received strength to conceive seed, and she bore a child when she was past the age, because she judged Him faithful who had promised" (Hebrews 11:11 NKJ). If you read the biography of Sarah throughout the Book of Genesis, you'll find that it took her a while to learn to trust God without trying to help Him along. But ultimately she too found out that God will do what He promises.

Our faith in His promises need never waver. God even gives us a promise about His promises: "Let us hold unswervingly to the hope we profess, for he who promised is faithful" (Hebrews 10:23).

But how can you really make the promises your own?

First, you have to find them. What a royal treasure hunt! Someone took the time to count the promises and found 7,464 of them.

In the margin of my Bible, next to 1 Kings 8:56 ("Not one word has failed of all the good promises he gave"), I have written: Study His promises so you know what you can claim!

As you read the Bible look especially for the words *will* and *shall:*

"Call upon me and come and pray to me, and I *will* listen to you" (Jeremiah 29:12).

"He that heareth my word, and believeth on him that sent me, hath everlasting life, and *shall not* come into condemnation; but is passed from death unto life" (John 5:24 KJV).

"God is faithful, who will not allow you to be tempted beyond what you are able, but with the temptation *will* also make the way of escape" (1 Corinthians 10:13 NKJ).

Other promises are simply strong affirmations using the words *is* or *are:*

"If any man be in Christ, he *is* a new creature: old things *are* passed away . . . all things *are* become new" (2 Corinthians 5:17 KJV).

"The Lord your God *is* with you wherever you go" (Joshua 1:9 NKJ).

"The prayer of a righteous man *is* powerful and effective" (James 5:16).

Still other promises are exciting declarations:

"The Lord upholds all those who fall and lifts up all who are bowed down" (Psalm 145:14).

"All things work together for good to those who love God" (Romans 8:28 NKJ).

"Cast all your anxiety on him . . . he cares for you" (1 Peter 5:7).

Second, once you've found the promises, make them easy to find again.

When I find a promise in the Bible (whether a phrase or an entire verse), I underline it. In one of my Bibles I started color coding the promise verses, lightly coloring over them with a blue pencil so I could find them at a glance. Sometimes I write the word *promise* beside the verse or make a letter *p* and circle it. I haven't found all 7,464 yet, but I'm looking.

Awhile ago I started making a notebook of promises so I could refer to them easily, but I could never find the notebook when I needed it. So I started a card file using an old recipe card box and some 3 x 5 index cards. I went through my Bible looking for verses I had colored blue. Then I typed one verse per card, sometimes using the back to note the wording of a different version of the Bible if it was particularly meaningful. Dividers separate the verses into categories.

Now when I'm having trouble with a particular sin in my life, I can look under the forgiveness category and find an appropriate promise: "If we confess our sins, he is faithful and just and will forgive us our sins and purify us from all unrighteousness" (1 John 1:9).

When I'm worried about tight finances, I can look under "care" and find a verse like Philippians 4:19: "God *will* meet all your needs according to his glorious riches in Christ Jesus."

As temptations come, I can find a promise like James 4:7: "Submit yourselves . . . to God. Resist the devil, and he *will* flee from you" (KJV).

When I feel totally inadequate to help my children with a difficult situation, I look under "wisdom" and find James 1:5: "If any of you lacks wisdom, he should ask God, who gives generously to all . . . and it *will* be given to him."

It is so exciting to know that God really cares about every situation and that He has given us His word that He will act on our behalf!

With the verses on 3 x 5 cards, I can easily carry them with me to memorize in spare moments. Most of us know how boring it is to have to wait in a doctor's examining room when we have forgotten to bring the magazine from the waiting room. What a good opportunity to store promises in our mental filing cabinets. Then the promise is there when we need it. We can call it to mind, tell God we're claiming it, and then believe that He will do what He has promised. Rest in it. A rainbow promise can brighten even the gloomiest day!

Deuteronomy 6:9 talks about writing God's words upon the posts of our house and on our gates. Sometimes I'll put an especially meaningful or appropriate promise on the refrigerator: "I can do everything [including say no to snacks] through him who gives me strength" (Philippians 4:13) or on the wall above the sink: "Let us not become weary in doing good, for at the proper time we will reap a harvest if we do not give up" (Galatians 6:9).

There's only one problem about plugging into the promises of Scripture. Not all of them are for me. I've found four basic types: personal, universal, conditional, and unconditional.

Personal promises are just that—specific promises to one person in Scripture meant exclusively for him or her. They are not for everyone to claim. For example, Sarah, Abraham's wife, was ninety years old when God spoke to Abraham and promised him that his wife would become pregnant. At ninety? That's what God said. God promised that Sarah's child would become the father of a mighty nation! That was an incredible promise! But God kept His word.

It was a personal promise, though, intended only for Sarah and Abraham. If I lived to be ninety years old and didn't have any children, I couldn't claim that promise (even if my name happened to be Sarah). God's promise, in this instance, was a private covenant between a special couple and Himself.

Universal promises, on the other hand, are for everyone. Probably the best-known example of a universal promise is John 3:16: "For God so loved the world, that he gave his only begotten Son, that whosoever believeth in him should not perish, but have everlasting life" (KJV). Those words apply to all. Many people around the world have come to faith in Christ through those precious words.

Galatians 6:7 is another universal promise: "Whatever a man sows, that he will also reap"

(NKJ). That applies to engineers as well as farmers, Christians and non-Christians, men and women, young and old. God will hold us responsible for our actions.

If I spend all my free time watching television or reading books that are not God-honoring, I cannot expect to reap a life of spiritual maturity. But if my leisure time is spent reading Christian literature, listening to uplifting music, and planting deeds of kindness in the lives of others, my Christian faith is bound to grow.

Conditional promises are the "if . . . then" type. "If you ask anything in My name, I will do it" (John 14:14 NKJ) is one that I have to be reminded about periodically. All too often, I stew over a problem and forget that God says He will act *if* I will pray about it.

Sometimes the "if . . . then" of the promise is not stated, but implied. There is a condition that we must meet before we can claim the promise. "Call upon me in the day of trouble [that's the condition]; [then] I will deliver you, and you will honor me" (Psalm 50:15).

Unconditional promises have no strings attached. "Being confident of this, that he who began a good work in you will carry it on to completion until the day of Christ Jesus" (Philippians 1:6). I'm glad His work in me doesn't depend on *my* being a certain way. I fail. I fall down. I sometimes give up. What a comfort to know He's still there, patiently working in me.

Not every promise in Scripture is for us, but most of them are. We're only handicapping ourselves if we're not making use of them. Study the verses surrounding the promise to determine which type it is. If it is one you can claim, take it for your own.

In a time when nothing seems sure, we all need something we can count on (besides death and taxes). We *can* count on God's promises.

One of my favorites is specifically spoken to women (although not exclusively, I'm sure). "Blessed is she who has believed that what the Lord has said to her will be accomplished!" (Luke 1:45). That was said of Mary, who had just accepted God's challenge to become mother to the Savior of the world. But it is stated in such a way that it is an affirmation to every woman (man and child) who believes in the God of rainbow promises.

Whether you organize a filing system or simply mark the promises in your Bible, the important thing is that you become aware that the promises are there. Memorize them. Use them. Meditate on them, and make them an important part of your life. Allow them to *transform* your life. That's how you plug into God's rainbow!

"The Lord is faithful to all his promises and loving toward all he has made" (Psalm 145:13).

(Hey, that's another one!)